DARK

ART

THE CHANGING FACE OF
PUBLIC RELATIONS

TIM BURT

First published 2012 by
Elliott and Thompson Limited
27 John Street, London WC1N 2BX
www.eandtbooks.com

ISBN: 978-1-907642-56-2

9 8 7 6 5 4 3 2 1

A CIP catalogue record for this book is available from the British Library.

Printed and bound in the UK by CPI Group (UK) Ltd, Croydon CR0 4YY

Typeset by Marie Doherty

For Helen

CONTENTS

INTRODUCTION

David Grigson, the finance director of Reuters, was late. Around the conference room, on the 5th floor of the group's London headquarters, there was a banker, the director of corporate affairs and the in-house legal counsel. The voice of Niall FitzGerald, the non-executive chairman, was issuing instructions over the conference call line – his quick-fire Irish patter audible to everyone.

Grigson rushed in. He shuffled his papers, which outlined the terms of an $18 billion bid for Reuters from Thomson Corporation, and looked around the board table. He went white and wide-eyed. Interrupting his chairman, he pointed my way and shouted: 'What on earth is he doing here?'

The Reuters finance director associated my face with the *Financial Times*, where I had been media editor for several years. Digging the dirt on Reuters had been a core part of the beat, scrutinising the company's arch rivalry with Bloomberg and its long-running transition from news agency to electronic data group. No one had told Grigson that I had crossed over. So far as he was concerned, a senior editorial writer had somehow infiltrated a secret discussion about the future sale of the company.

The corporate affairs director intervened. 'It's all right. Tim's now at Brunswick. He's helping us on the deal.' Grigson shook his head and grunted: 'Welcome to the dark side.'

In the corporate world, the 'dark side' has become the moniker for a shadowy industry that generates global revenues of more than $10 billion annually. Those revenues are earned by a disparate network of business and financial PR companies, which have multiplied rapidly over the past 30 years. Launched initially in the leading capital markets' centres of London, New York and Frankfurt, the largest firms now have tentacles in every city with any kind of growing business community.

From Atlanta to Zhejiang, firms have opened offices to help manage the public relations of companies large and small. These are the practitioners of what critics call the dark arts – the tactics employed to burnish corporate images or to protect companies from media vitriol.

For most of its history, the art of the financial PR industry was not that dark. It relied on a relatively simple and transparent model: to distribute a client's earnings announcements and to secure positive coverage in the press month-after-month, year-on-year.

The business equation was similarly straightforward. Each agency sought fees from enough retained clients to more than cover their costs. They then competed for the hugely profitable deal mandates that flowed with mergers and acquisitions. It made rich men of entrepreneurs such as Richard Edelman and Gershon Kekst, the eponymous leaders of their New York-based agencies, as well as Lord Bell of London's Bell Pottinger, Christoph Walther of Munich's CNC and Anne Meaux of Image Sept in Paris. Alan Parker, the chairman of Brunswick, is typical of the entrepreneurial pack. The firm he conceived with a couple of friends at his London kitchen table in 1987, now employs more than 600 people working in 20 offices around the world.

Leading agencies can enjoy multi-million dollar retained fees from individual global clients, exceeding $10 million a year in some cases. The payments are even richer in times of crisis and takeovers. For owner-controlled firms, such fees and the more modest retainers that pay most of the monthly bills have sustained an extremely comfortable lifestyle. Second homes and second wives are common. For the most successful, the trophies frequently include third homes, chauffeurs for the third car, fractional ownership in NetJets, and race horses or grouse moors for the weekend. To preserve their wealth, agency founders have reinvested heavily in expanding their businesses, building a network of offices from which to manage the media.

In some cases, that strategy persuaded firms to recruit aggressively from the media, seeking to strengthen their connections to the journalistic community.

In 2004, at my desk at the *Financial Times*, the telephone rang. 'I have Alan Parker for you,' said one of his three secretaries (two for business, one for social engagements). The ensuing conversation and subsequent meetings amounted to a corporate seduction. The chat-up line was relatively simple. 'We'd like you to replicate your *FT* trajectory on our side of the fence – help us internationalise our media offering; help us open offices in new markets; help us advise the sort of clients you write about.'

Brunswick's approach was well timed. The newspaper industry was just waking up to an existential threat that would, in the ensuing years, challenge its old business model. Costs were being cut throughout the media. Advertising revenues were tumbling. Morale was mixed, at best, in newsrooms. A career change, with an open invitation to return to the *FT*, seemed worth considering. A five-year stretch at Brunswick, one of the most successful financial PR agencies, offered a ringside seat to some of the largest takeover deals of the decade, along with behind-the-scenes roles in major corporate bust-ups, executive scandals and various corporate intrigues.

At the time of my departure, in June 2005, an *FT* spokesman told *MediaGuardian*: 'He isn't the first journalist to move in to PR and he won't be the last. Maybe one day he'll move back.' As that door closed, and another opened, Alan Parker warned: 'You have to be sure you have finished with journalism; we occupy a different world.'

In reality, journalism is never finished with you. That is why most of the reporters converting to public relations tend to apply their old editorial skills to their new trade: the ability to tell a good story; how to formulate thoughtful commentary; delivering succinct verdicts about a company; and the experience to predict how the media will cover things. As strategic consultants, they still rely on shorthand; still thrive on media gossip; still retain an eye for the main story. They just do it behind the scenes; from the dark side.

But the conversion from newsroom to agency, from high-visibility correspondent to low-profile consultant requires more than simply plying your old trade in a new suit. Predatory news instincts have to be abandoned. As a consultant, success depends on swapping an adversarial approach to business for unashamed advocacy. The transition is not easy. It requires a willingness to shed old prejudices; an ability to defend instead of prosecute.

Dark Art attempts to shine a light on the evolution of an industry rarely written about: financial and business public relations or, as it now often describes itself, strategic corporate communications. It offers a window on the world of media management, crisis planning, deal-making communications and the growing reliance on industry intelligence. It is part 'rough guide' to PR, part history album of the industry and part diagnosis of the new forces reshaping the market.

Today's communications consultant is a quite different operator than his predecessor. The old rules of patronage and favours – which sustained some agencies for years – are being replaced by a new meritocracy built around professional services. Traditional powers of persuasion have not been abandoned completely. But they are proving less effective in a rapidly globalising, increasingly digital corporate environment.

The 'wind of change' sweeping through public relations has its roots in the storm conditions battering other business sectors – from crisis-hit clients at one end of the corporate spectrum to loss-making media outlets at the other. Since the financial crisis of 2008, companies and their boards have become increasingly anxious about how quickly hard-built reputations can be shredded in a digitally connected world. The roll call of high profile corporations suffering PR meltdowns – from banking to the oil industry, from newspaper publishers to carmakers – has only heightened business anxiety.

The crisis cycle has coincided with a structural change in media consumption habits, defined by worsening newspaper economics and costly new distribution systems. Traditional media outlets, competing with new digital rivals, have become more opinionated and polemical in a twin bid to retain existing audiences and to secure new ones. Many business leaders see a direct linkage between a media industry struggling for survival and the shift towards greater risk-taking by reporters, and the rise of agenda journalism.

Whether it is real or not, the perceived behavioural change in the media has prompted new engagement tactics by the PR industry. The old way of doing things, the simple art of story placement, has been transformed into the communications equivalent of three-dimensional chess, in which clients and their advisers have to consider several moves ahead before making their opening play.

Yet in spite of the growing complexity and the emergence of new opinion formers, many chairmen and chief executives tend to agonise about only a few types of coverage, and largely in traditional media outlets. For some, their innate conservatism has proved their communications downfall. A discreet call to the editor of the *Wall Street Journal* can no longer spike a story. A quip to a TV reporter can go viral in a matter of seconds – haunting a chief executive to his eventual resignation. Tony Hayward, the former chief executive of BP, would testify to that. Companies in multiple sectors are desperate to avoid a Hayward moment, and they are demanding new sorts of communications advice with different sorts of outcomes.

Dark Art looks at an industry struggling to adjust. It explores what has gone wrong, and what might emerge in the next generation of strategic communications. It does not claim to have all the answers, or even to address all of the industry's shortcomings. But it examines some of the issues and the case histories of a business that rarely admits to health problems, and which does not like to self-diagnose.

This book would not have been possible without the support and encouragement that I enjoyed over five years at Brunswick – especially from Alan Parker and his co-founders Andrew Fenwick and Louise Charlton. Friends and colleagues there, and at numerous other agencies, have offered helpful advice and suggestions. Business leaders have been similarly generous with their time, including many who spoke on condition of anonymity, with useful insights and corrections. *Dark Art* also relies heavily on my 16 years as a business reporter, foreign correspondent and industry specialist at the *FT* – a rare newspaper to have survived and flourished in the multi-platform world. Reporters and editors at the *FT*, along with several other media outlets, have assisted with the text.

Dark Art would never have reached the book stores without the subsequent encouragement of my colleagues Philip Gawith and Julian Hanson-Smith at StockWell Group, the firm where I am now joint managing partner. Halfway through writing it, I shattered my shoulder in an accident. As with that incident, any error of judgment in *Dark Art* is mine alone. Any inaccuracies are likewise mine, with single-handed typing and voice-recognition software not offering any excuse. But the book has not been a single-handed effort. It would not have been possible without the support of friends and colleagues including Anthony Silverman, Suzanne Bartch, Robert Morgan, Borbala Nagy, Anushka Mathew, Chloe Maier, Kate Heighes and Lorraine Aziz. David Crundwell of Thomson Reuters deserves special thanks for introducing me to Olivia Bays, the unendingly patient mentor, editor and publisher at Elliott and Thompson in London.

The greatest thanks are due to Helen, my long-suffering partner, who has accompanied me from cub reporter to corporate adviser. When I contemplated leaving journalism for public relations, she advised sagely: 'Don't do it for the money.' As most authors of non-fiction can attest, a book like *Dark Art* is not written for the money.

PART ONE

The Great Persuaders

CHAPTER I

The Age of Anxiety

The first decade of the twenty-first century ended with a series of corporate calamities that shook the confidence of boards and their shareholders.

In short order, the world's most successful investment bank was threatened by questions over its role in the global financial crisis. The largest automotive group was undermined by an unprecedented vehicle recall, prompted by a consumer outcry over alleged safety problems. And one of the most profitable oil producers was hit by a massive spill off the coast of its most important market.

In each case, the communications response to the corporate maladies made things worse, not better, at Goldman Sachs, at Toyota Motor Corporation and at BP. Consumer confidence in business conduct, already shaky following the collapse of Lehman Brothers in 2008 and still fragile amid a continuing sub-prime mortgage crisis, was dealt a further blow. The series of crises, which continued into 2011 and 2012, exposed serious shortcomings in the communications planning and preparation at several leading businesses. It also raised questions about the capabilities of their costly PR advisers, hired to contain media criticism and wider consumer discontent in times of trouble.

In PR terms, the end of one decade and the beginning of the next marked a new age of anxiety, when company boards feared for their reputations. Directors everywhere wanted to know: how to avoid being the next BP. The oil giant was tarnished by the 2010 oil spill that has since become a case study in how to lose a reputation.

The Deepwater Horizon accident, involving the death of 11 oil rig workers, reverberated in the global media, alarming other companies exposed to major industrial risk. Unlike the

Exxon Valdez oil disaster of 1989, this was the first major spill of the digital age. The combination of TV footage from the ocean floor, vivid images of stained wildlife and a US media consumed with the devastation to local communities made BP public enemy number one. It was the first corporate crisis played out in real time, spawning a worldwide digital debate about business trust and ethics, and leapt quickly from the business pages of newspapers on to the front pages and then into television prime time.

BP was unprepared. 'There was chaos and confusion inside the company because there were few contingency plans of how to deal with it,' according to one PR adviser involved in the crisis. 'No one imagined that the safety back-ups would fail. Such a scenario was described in BP's risk register as a low probability high impact event.'

Another person involved in trying to repair BP's reputation recalls: 'There wasn't a good crisis communications handbook. What BP did have in terms of a crisis plan stayed in a drawer.'

The reputational damage was compounded by the Obama administration's decision publicly to chastise the company. Facing mid-term elections, the President was keen to avoid the same damage to the White House that President George W. Bush had suffered in the aftermath of Hurricane Katrina. So the story, initially a serious environmental accident, became a major political one. In an unprecedented intervention, President Obama suggested that he would have sacked Tony Hayward if he had had the power to do so.

Every PR effort to demonstrate BP's clean-up commitment was undermined by engineering setbacks. The rising tide of US anger and media criticism escalated when attempts to cap the leaking Macondo well failed. It descended into farce when a 'junk shot' of shredded tyres and old golf balls was fired into the well. By then, even golfing magazines were laying siege to BP's PR machine, keen to know what brand of balls were being used.

Almost 90 days after the initial rig explosion, the Macondo well was sealed. But by that time, more than $100 billion had been wiped off BP's market capitalisation, and the company had set aside $40 billion for compensation.

For BP, it was a near-death experience. Midway through the crisis, according to one BP insider: 'Markets took fright at potentially unlimited liabilities. Our debt became illiquid. The environmental disaster risked becoming a financial one. There was a scramble for cash inside the company; the Treasury department worked around the clock to save it.'

BP was saved – at significant cost. Tony Hayward was not. Announcing his resignation, barely ten days after oil stopped leaking, Hayward said: 'I believe the decision I have reached with the board to step down is consistent with the responsibility BP has shown throughout these terrible events. BP will be a changed company as a result of Macondo and it is right that it should embark on its next phase under new leadership.'

Privately, Hayward felt a victim. He later told one colleague: 'I stepped off the pavement and got hit by a bus.' He is said by friends to nurse a lingering, deeply held antipathy to the media in all shapes and forms.

The lessons were far-reaching, according to those involved in the reputation-recovery work. 'The biggest PR warning was to show that companies have to think about their reputational exposure in what we call peace-time. In the heat of the battle, when a company is in trauma, it is too late to start educating people about what is good about your response strategy,' says one BP veteran.

Barely had the well been capped before companies large and small began to commission reports on how to enhance their own crisis communications. Although PR had been seen as part of BP's problem, agencies elsewhere sensed an opportunity to sell a new kind of service: how to prepare for and avoid a Macondo-style trauma.

The services focused on improved crisis rehearsal and the need to develop a detailed communications handbook on how to behave towards multiple audiences including regulators, politicians through to customers, suppliers and consumers. It was also clear from BP that companies in crisis should not always deploy their chief executive as 'chief communicator' because, as Tony Hayward found to his cost, they are often ill-equipped to deal with the media.

At BP, there were well-developed risk policies. The group crisis handbook recommends that a single steering group should be formed to run the entire response effort. But BP did not create such a group until well into the Deepwater Horizon disaster. By that point the US coastguard had assumed control of a clean-up operation involving more than 200 different organisations and 30 call centres.

As the crisis unfolded, the PR industry watched with a mixture of despair and alarm as tried and tested tactics failed to stem the criticism. TV appearances, town hall meetings, press conference apologies – nothing reduced the clamour. It was a turning point for PR.

In spite of BP's public humiliation, several other companies did not embrace the PR lessons, or learn how to alleviate acute reputation anxiety. Within a year, similar anxiety attacks hit McKinsey, Nokia, Tepco, Blackberry, Netflix, HP, News Corp and Olympus. Other companies felt pre-judged by the media and suffered reputational damage when they were later found not to be at fault.

Toyota, the Japanese carmaker, publicly apologised and announced a major set of reforms following massive vehicle recalls in 2009–10 in response to allegedly faulty accelerators, brakes and other components. In February 2011, the company would eventually be exonerated by safety bodies and regulators in the USA. But the damage was already done. Toyota was judged guilty by parts of the media well before the official investigations were complete. Toyota whistle-blowers fed the media, as did industry rivals, consumer groups, class-action lawyers and politicians. The furore threatened to destabilise the entire strategy laid down by Akio Toyoda, the first member of the carmaker's founding family to lead the company in generations.

On 9 March 2011 – eighteen months after the recalls began – Toyota attempted to draw a line under the affair. The company president cut the size of Toyota's cumbersome board by more than half. He removed an entire layer of management, and set up an independent advisory committee to monitor quality controls. Insiders vowed that they would not allow the brand to lose a PR battle again.

Whether the reputational damage was unjustified or not, most of the corporate crises of recent years have been characterised by a lack of readiness for the ensuing media circus. And companies were unprepared for the impact on their share prices as investors took fright at potential liabilities.

The corporate crises of 2010–11 wiped more than €170 billion off the market capitalisation of the businesses affected, according to investor research which calculated that the value destruction far exceeded the pervading stock market volatility. Amid such value destruction, many company executives blame the media – particularly the social media – for rushing to judgment before the true cause of the problems has been investigated. Some communications spokesmen talk regretfully about having to 'feed the beast'. Others despair at the pack mentality of a media sector hunting for the next scoop. This PR lament is even louder among companies that, for whatever reason, have fallen from grace.

Nowhere has that fall been faster and harder than at News Corp, the global media empire led by Rupert Murdoch.

A business built up over generations has been dealt a hammer blow by illegal phone-hacking commissioned by its disgraced former tabloid flagship: the *News of the World*. Responding to the crisis, News Corp closed one of its few reliably profitable newspapers. It jettisoned its UK publishing chief executive; accepted the resignation of the head of Dow Jones; and saw a clutch of employees past and present arrested. In 2011, the group's ageing chairman and his heir apparent, James Murdoch, were verbally caned by a parliamentary select committee, and then faced even more intimate scrutiny less than a year later from the Leveson Inquiry into UK media standards.

'Mr Murdoch has looked lost,' reported Philip Stephens in the *Financial Times* of 11 November 2011. 'Too slow to grasp the significance when the dam burst, he has been at once contrite, dismissive and irritable. You can see what he must be thinking. After half a century of labour, is this how it ends?'

The scale of the reputational damage was acknowledged by the octogenarian News Corp chairman in a full-page newspaper advertisement carried by seven British newspapers in July 2011. In it, Murdoch wrote: 'We are sorry. The *News of the World* was in the business of holding others to account. It failed when it came to itself. We are sorry for the serious wrong-doing that occurred. We are deeply sorry for the hurt suffered by individuals affected. We regret not acting faster to sort things out.'

It was not a time for public relations. It was the moment for public regret.

Mr Murdoch's contrition ranked among the more extraordinary recent *mea culpas* by chief executives. A collection of other corporate apologies, compiled by The Street on 14 October 2011, the US business media website, quoted similarly humble words from Mike Lazaridis of Research in Motion, Reed Hastings at Netflix, Lloyd C. Blankfein of Goldman Sachs and, of course, Tony Hayward at BP.

Amid the reputational wreckage of Deepwater Horizon, Hayward even had to apologise for an apology. It was the nadir of his PR exposure. At the end of May 2010, Hayward caused uproar for qualifying how sorry he was to a US TV reporter, by adding: 'There's no one who wants this over more than I do. I'd like my life back.'

By the following Wednesday, 2 June, Hayward had to apologise again, admitting: 'I made a hurtful and thoughtless comment on Sunday when I said that I wanted my life back. When I read that recently, I was appalled. I apologize, especially to the families of the 11 men who lost their lives in this tragic accident.

Those words don't represent how I feel about this tragedy, and certainly don't represent the hearts of the people of BP – many of whom live and work in the Gulf – who are doing everything they can to make things right.'

The apologies, scripted and unscripted, were symptomatic of a growing anxiety over the risks posed to hard-won business reputations. They also represented an admission of collective failure by many companies that their crisis communications plans were not ready for the digital age, where constant online scrutiny has sharply reduced reaction times.

Such threats are hardly new, as observers of BCCI, Polly Peck, Mirror Group, Pan Am, Enron and Arthur Andersen would testify. No amount of PR could have saved those companies. But even healthy companies now feel exposed. Rising profits and revenues can help to defend a reputation, but they are no longer a guarantee of respectability. Many companies have begun to review the quality of the advice they have traditionally relied upon.

The growing threat prompted the chairman of Britain's Institute of Directors (IoD), Neville Bain, to urge company boards to attach a higher priority to reputation management. Calling for more concerted action, he cited Benjamin Franklin's warning that: 'It takes many good deeds to build a good reputation, and only one bad one to lose it.'

In June 2011, the IoD issued a report in collaboration with the Chartered Institute of Public Relations with a dozen recommendations on enhancing reputation planning and minimising risk. In doing so, the two business associations presaged a subtle, major and potentially lucrative shift in the advisory services provided to leading companies.

'Senior public relations/communications professionals should take an active part in strategic planning so that reputational opportunities and risks can inform decision-making,' according to one recommendation. 'This is a different approach to that of expecting the public relations professional to manage the impacts of strategic decisions that have already been made by the board, without considering reputation explicitly.'

This exhortation has been taken up enthusiastically by PR agencies. In the absence of much mergers and acquisitions (M&A) activity and a thin pipeline for initial public offerings (IPOs), crisis work helped pay the bonuses and fill the incentive pools for some of the largest firms in the communications industry.

'Crisis is the new M&A' has become a common refrain among PR leaders. For some agencies, crisis and reputation risk management became a vital earnings stream in 2010 and 2011, and continues to be so in 2012. It has certainly become one of the most important revenue streams for firms on both sides of the Atlantic. Edelman, the US agency, was called in to support News Corp. Bell Pottinger, its London-based rival, was contracted to support government organisations from Sri Lanka to Bahrain. Brunswick acted for both BP and Toyota. Collectively, they and other agencies earned generous fees from crisis mandates. For some, the revenues were running at several million dollars per month.

The crises also marked a watershed for agencies that had previously focused on one discipline, such as financial public relations, product marketing, investor relations or public affairs. Suddenly, they had to adapt to attacks that spanned every area of a client's reputation, posing a threat to the jobs of numerous chief executives, alarming investors and arousing the ire of consumers, regulators and politicians. This new broader scope to PR has coincided with a cyclical change in client sentiment.

Alan Parker, founder and chairman of Brunswick, one of the agencies to capitalise on the crisis upturn, summed up the change in approach. In the *Brunswick Review*, distributed to the firm's clients at the end of 2010, Parker wrote: 'It is always more difficult to manage and communicate when times are hard; and how management responds defines its reputation. In this challenging environment it is easy for management to see only increased hostility and risk. But we believe there is never a better time to communicate a company's vision and aspirations'.

In reality, the events at Toyota, BP, News Corp, McKinsey and others have tended to make senior business leaders risk averse, and less willing to communicate. But in a digital era, a say-nothing approach poses a major risk. Other commentators will fill the vacuum. The crisis years have posed a threat not only to famous corporations but also to the entire service proposition of PR. An industry that thought it was indispensible has had to reassert itself. It has had to justify its existence.

The industry now insists that its advisory capabilities – following BP and other calamaties – are now more relevant than ever. PR veterans warn that the challenge is not whether to communicate, but how. For most of the past century, financial PR advice was limited to controlling the earnings messaging and managing the print media. In the second decade of the new century, such tactics have been found wanting. It has prompted a realisation among boardrooms, in-house PR leaders and PR agencies themselves that the old ways of communicating have to change.

CHAPTER 2

The Feudal System

In the mid-1980s, the chairman of a leading international company was alerted to a potentially damning story about his private life that a Sunday newspaper intended to publish. Concerned at the damage to his profile, the chairman called his retained PR advisers.

Within an hour, one of the PR firm's young executives was dispatched to the Sunday newspaper's offices. His job was clear but challenging: retrieve any compromising pictures of the client-company's chairman.

The PR man walked to the back of the newspaper offices, where newsprint was being delivered in huge rolls for the presses that in those days still occupied the same building as the editorial staff. Having blagged his way through the delivery entrance, the executive found his way, along passages and up stairways, to the newsroom. Claiming to be a temporary sub-editor working a shift, he found his way to the picture desk, where he asked for the film proofs of his client. The picture editor, assuming he was liaising with the back-bench on page layout, handed them over. The PR executive made his way out of the building. This time he walked audaciously through the main entrance. The pictures never appeared.

Back in the 1980s, this sort of bravado was one way to demonstrate client loyalty. It reflected what corporate bosses expected from agencies, which they treated like old retainers. This duty of loyalty, and the risks taken by advisers in their client's cause, owed less to professional marketing services than to old-style feudalism.

Traditional feudalism, dating back to the Norman Conquest, was founded on the principle of land grants in return for armed service and loyalty unto death. Before long, with land and loyalty in short supply, England's nobility found it more convenient to pay financial 'indentures of retainer'. Charles Plummer, the nineteenth-century historian, coined the phrase 'bastard feudalism' to describe how medieval aristocracy started paying cash-for-favours instead of offering land to vassals. By the 1980s it neatly captured the bonds of public relations. Under Plummer's useful metaphor for the PR industry, feudalism was thus bastardised into retained contracts based on 'loyalty for as long as it pays'.[1]

Most old-school PR gurus would plead ignorance about bastard feudalism. But had such PR advisers existed in the Dark Ages, they would have joined retinues including judges, mercenaries, courtiers and the clergy. Retained priests could be especially useful when divine intervention was deemed helpful.

Fast-forward several hundred years and some PR leaders still liken their role to priesthood: counselling, explaining codes of conduct and advising on best behaviour. At least three leaders of UK agencies have considered taking holy orders or even trained as priests. Lord Chadlington, the PR baron and chairman of Huntsworth (a firm representing more than 600 clients), is one such convert. In December 2011, he told BBC Radio 4's *Today* programme: 'I don't think the step from being a priest to being a PR man is that different. Because in one sense you are persuading people; you are thinking about a message; you are selling it as hard as you can do, and that is what both roles involve.'

For most of the last century, PR was built on the simple tasks of salesmanship and persuasion, underpinned by feudal loyalty to clients.

The PR industry's adoption of such principles was first analysed in the 1920s by Edward Bernays, a former special adviser to US President Woodrow Wilson. After serving on the US Committee on Public Information during the First World War, Bernays turned his attention to lucrative corporate clients, advising companies including Procter & Gamble and Alcoa.

---

[1] Juliet Gardiner and Neil Wenborn (eds.), *The History Today Companion to British History*, London, Collins & Brown, 1995.

Bernays back then, like Lord Chadlington today, saw public relations as a vital intermediary between business and ordinary consumers. Writing in 1928, he laid the foundations for corporate communications when he analysed how public relations should meld psychology, salesmanship and propaganda. Business, Bernays wrote, 'must explain itself, its aims, its objectives, to the public in terms which the public can understand and is willing to accept ... it is this condition and necessity which has created the need for a specialized field of public relations'.

The Bernays model, set out in his book *Propaganda*,[2] earned him the title 'father of public relations'. In it, he acknowledged the feudal loyalties of the industry, adding: 'Business now calls in the public relations counsel to advise it, to interpret its purpose to the public, and to suggest those modifications which may make it conform to public demand.'

The 'father of PR' urged all 'successful propagandists' to portray business as a public good, delivering more than just profit and shareholder returns. Every company had to be a business of repute, creating a groundswell of goodwill and customer support. The Austrian-American publicist was remarkably prescient, especially given the crises that would overwhelm companies such as BP and Lehman Brothers 80 years later. 'An oil corporation which truly understands its many-sided relation to the public, will offer that public not only good oil but a sound labor policy,' Bernays wrote, 'A bank will seek to show not only that its management is sound and conservative, but also that its officers are honorable both in their public and in their private life.'

His thinking was influenced heavily by psychoanalysis, a field to which Bernays was first exposed by his uncle, Sigmund Freud. Using Freudian methods, he deduced that public relations depended on managing 'psychological and emotional currents'.

As the dynasty behind both the father of psychoanalysis and the father of public relations, it is not surprising that

---

[2] E.L. Bernays, *Propaganda*, New York, Ig Publishing, 2004 (first published by Horace Liveright, 1928).

communication techniques continued to run in the family. That mantle has been inherited, and continues to be refined today, by Matthew Freud, head of the eponymous London-based PR agency.

Rather like Bernays and his great-grandfather Sigmund, the younger Freud sees his role as solving problems for retained clients. In some respects, Freud has adopted the image of PR adviser as corporate therapist, counselling his clients through tough decisions. Sounding more like a shrink than a communications guru, he told one interviewer, in *Management Today*, February 2009: 'I get to talk to interesting people who have interesting problems. They may be CEOs, but they're surprisingly isolated. They're surrounded by people who work for them. They're also isolated by their sector.'

Freud, who is married to Rupert Murdoch's daughter Elisabeth, personifies PR feudalism. Charming and intimidating in equal measure, Matthew cajoles, harries and seeks favours on behalf of his clients. In return, they pay him lucrative retainers that sustain an agency of more than 200 people catering for clients including PepsiCo, Carphone Warehouse and Nike.

Feudal duty to long-standing clients has also shaped other agencies – including Finsbury and Brunswick in the UK and Kekst, Abernathy MacGregor and Edelman in the USA. By promising absolute client loyalty, such firms have secured a lucrative role as both gatekeepers and consiglieri to chairmen and chief executives around the world. Yet Freud says: 'I've got almost no influence in my own right. The people I represent are genuinely influential. But if I'm joining the dots, it's not for me or my benefit but for the mutual benefit of other people.'

The real power of such agency founders lies in their access to business leaders – the feudal overlords – who pay for reputation management. In turn, this system relies on a powerful extended network of patronage, which helps to bring in new business.

As with the feudalism, the use of patronage by the PR industry has parallels in medieval power-broking. In the USA and UK, the launch of new PR firms in the 1980s and 1990s owed much to the support of business leaders who inserted their favourite advisers into every company they joined. In a competitive market for clients, agency leaders pursued businessmen who advanced their cause, just as courtiers and liverymen did hundreds of years ago.

The historian L.C.B. Seaman, describing the patronage system, might have been explaining PR networking when he wrote: 'Any man who wished to advance his career and protect his interest [had] to find a great noble to provide him with their "good lordship". Some men were sufficiently concerned for their interests to accept retainer fees from two or three different lords without necessarily performing any particular service for any of them.'

In the late twentieth century, the system of PR patronage proved mutually beneficial to both client and agency. In addition to earning a retainer, a well-connected PR executive hoped to gain influence from his or her association with a powerful patron. The patron, in turn, expected to rely on his servant's growing circle of influence to protect him when needed. The historical version of patronage, as defined by Seaman, has a further application to public relations by acknowledging that 'in the relations between patron and client, as traditionally in those between master and servant, the "exploitation" and advantage were not always as one-sided as they seem.'[3]

Corporate patronage helped launch several agencies. Alan Parker, the founder and chairman of Brunswick, has depended on influential patrons such as David Mayhew, the former chairman of J.P. Morgan Cazenove, and John Varley of Barclays. The same is true of many leading agencies in other countries, particularly in the close-knit world of New York firms and in the industrial economies of mainland Europe. For example, Peje Emilsson, chairman of Kreab Gavin Anderson in Sweden,

---

[3] L.C.B. Seaman, *A New History of England 410–1975*, Brighton, Harvester Press, 1981.

has long benefited from being a trusted retainer to Jacob Wallenberg, head of Scandinavia's most influential industrial dynasty. Similarly, Christoph Walther of the German agency CNC was introduced by his patron, industrialist Wolfgang Reitzle, to industrialists who might be helpful in business.

Roland Rudd, founder of RLM Finsbury, the Anglo-American agency, is another product of the patronage system. Numerous doors have been opened for Rudd by patrons including Sir Roger Carr, chairman of Centrica and a plural non-executive director; Lord Mandelson, the former government minister and one-time European Commissioner; and Sir Martin Sorrell, chief executive of WPP, the world's largest marketing group. Sir Martin adopted the same approach to Finsbury as the legendary Victor Kiam did to Remington. He liked it so much he bought the company.

If Edward Bernays fathered the rise of such propagandists in the USA, with their affinity to feudal patronage, then John Addey applied the model in Britain. In the 1960s, Addey formed one of the first dedicated City PR firms, built on the principle of securing influence and managing the media. From his apartment in Piccadilly, Addey intermediated between business and the media, trusted by both.

Tim Jackaman, former chairman of Square Mile Communications, in *Management Today*, I February 2000, said: 'As far as I'm concerned, all the thoroughbred horses in this industry have come from one stallion ... and that stallion is John Addey. He really invented the whole genre of financial PR. He was a very successful chap, as sharp as anything and charming too. Importantly, he had a good head for figures and ran a line between clients and journalists brilliantly. In his heyday he was a colossus.'

Addey taught his method of power and patronage to Brian Basham, a former financial journalist among the first to swap the newsroom for the advisory sector – crossing to the 'dark side'. Basham, who formed Broad Street Associates in the 1970s, likewise tutored Alan Parker as his deputy. 'I taught Alan the lesson of control,' said Basham. 'We developed a very powerful position for financial PRs where we came to be seen as controllers of a very valuable commodity: company news.'

Having learned his trade at Basham's knee, Parker formed Brunswick in the late 1980s – but not before considering joining forces with a group of entrepreneurs who subsequently set up Financial Dynamics, another firm spawned in the heady days of City deregulation and busy takeovers. It was an era of few rules, and even fewer ways to measure effectiveness. So for years, the financial PR machine was able to rely on the untested claim that it could manage the media better than most companies' in-house communications teams.

Businessmen anxious for favourable headlines bought into that promise. They agreed, in effect, to outsource large parts of their communications work to firms promising a good press. And the PR industry's gatekeeper status was enhanced by the media itself. Reporters under pressure to produce scoops and put stories in context began to rely more and more on the PR machine to feed them useful bits of information and exclusive stories.

This symbiotic relationship enabled agencies formed in the 1980s and 1990s to trade on a perception of access and influence. With few checks and balances on their services, agencies sold what amounted to communications insurance to their patrons.

Like car or household insurance, a number of clients rather resented paying the hefty premiums, and frequently doubted the value of what they were getting. But they paid up because they sensed that everyone needed insurance. And they hoped they would see the value in the regrettable event of a corporate car crash or house fire.

The payback was relatively simple for the agencies working this model. Under the corporate feudal system, PR firms hoped that the combined 'insurance retainers' would more than cover their operating costs. Once such costs were met, the fees for one-off projects – particularly mergers and acquisitions – flowed straight through to the bottom line. In the heady days of the takeover boom, fortunes were made.

For the most successful agencies, their chairmen became as wealthy as the corporate barons who retained them. The old master–servant relationship became increasingly blurred. Influential agency bosses such as Gershon Kekst, chairman of the New York firm bearing his name, became power-brokers in their own right. In the ruling executive class, they were useful allies in both acquiring and preserving boardroom power.

Today, there are chairmen and chief executives of numerous Fortune 500 companies who owe their longevity partly to the lobbying efforts and influence of their external PR advisers. Some agency chairmen can open the doors to new roles; others exercise influence in the heart of government to help win favours – or claim to.

Grateful corporate bosses often pay up because they now owe their PR consigliere a debt of loyalty. So the feudal relationship can be inverted, depending on who is the debtor, and who holds real power. In PR, such debts are particularly valuable when firms work pro bono to protect the reputation of an outgoing chairman or chief executive. In such cases, agencies waive their normal fees, gambling that they will be repaid handsomely when the indebted business leader secures their next role.

Thus, the old feudal structure, the traditional basis of retainers for influence, has evolved into a mutually dependent, mutually beneficial business relationship. But the system is under strain, threatened by a combination of disenchantment at sky-high fees, as well as a growing need for legal compliance, along with increased competence of in-house counsel and tougher regulation. The damaging impact when the media exposes feudal largesse from the boardroom has further strained the old ways of doing business. Those methods have also been found lacking at times of major corporate crises, ranging in recent years from BP to News Corp. Today, no amount of old favours and backroom influence can fully mitigate an industrial disaster or boardroom in-fighting, particularly when played out in the glare of digital media.

In the twenty-first century, what Edward Bernays termed the 'successful propagandists' have begun to rethink their approach once again. The old model has struggled to meet a basic feudal obligation: it is no longer able to manage the media.

CHAPTER 3

Managing the Media

In March 1945, my grandfather turned down rival offers of senior editorial roles from Lord Kemsley, owner of the *Sunday Times*, and Lord Beaverbrook, the legendary proprietor of Express Newspapers.

By then, Beaverbrook was Lord Privy Seal, a member of Winston Churchill's inner cabinet. The 'Beaver', as he was known by friends and colleagues, had recruited my grandfather two years earlier as a ministerial adviser on air transport – forcing him to leave the *Sunday Times*, and his role as the only British war correspondent embedded with the US Army 8th Air Force in its daylight raids over Europe.

With the end of the war in sight, the *Sunday Times* wanted him back. And the Beaver wanted him for the *Express*. He rejected both, instead becoming a diplomat in Washington DC, and later an industrialist. Beaverbrook, one of the most hands-on media managers, questioned his decision but nevertheless 'dictated a generous piece for the Evening Standard'.[4]

The ability of such media proprietors to dictate the news long pre-dated Beaverbrook, and has remained a surreptitious practice by newspaper owners ever since. Such magnates have always derived power from their ability to shape coverage in their own media, bestowing favourable stories on their political and business allies, or destroying reputations among their enemies.

Nowhere is that power more concentrated than in the slightly shambling, irascible frame of Keith Rupert Murdoch, chairman of News Corp, one of the world's largest media empires. Rupert Murdoch's reputation, and that of his newspaper operations, was damaged severely in 2011 by revelations of industrial-scale phone-hacking by journalists at the *News of the*

---

[4] Sir Peter Masefield, *Flight Path*, Shrewsbury, Airlife, 2002.

World – a story that Murdoch titles barely covered until it was fully exposed by rival investigative reporters.

In spite of the scandal, the closure of the *News of the World* and the ongoing investigations, Murdoch remains a revered figure. 'He is probably the most influential and powerful media figure in the world,' according to veteran Australian reporter Neil Chenoweth. 'His empire triggers effects directly and indirectly across the globe far beyond the size of his company. He wields this power unfettered by other shareholders or bankers or independent directors or even by national governments. He hasn't achieved this power by accident. While he is a great media man, he is first of all a great businessman.'[5]

His power and influence was coveted by business-leaders and politicians, many of whom would queue up for an audience – at least in the days preceding the phone-hacking scandal. David Cameron, the British prime minister, was often front of the queue.

'There was never a party, a breakfast, a lunch, a cuppa or a drink that Cameron & Co would not turn up to in force if The Great Man was there,' said Kelvin Mackenzie, the former editor of Murdoch's flagship tabloid, *The Sun*, in the *Evening Standard* on 12 October 2011, 'An American with a disdain for Britain, running a declining industry in terms of sales, profitability and influence, was considered more important than a meeting with any captain of industry no matter how big their workforce or balance sheet.'

In reality, some captains of industry were just as keen as the British prime minister to secure Murdoch's favour, perhaps hoping for benign treatment by News Corp titles such as the *Wall Street Journal* or *The Times*. Very few succeeded, either because they failed to connect with 'KRM', as internal memos to Murdoch are titled, or because they failed to hold his attention. 'He's listening to you, but you know he's having at least a

---

[5] Neil Chenoweth, *Rupert Murdoch: The Untold Story of the World's Greatest Media Wizard*, New York, Crown Business, 2001.

dozen mental conversations of his own at the same time,' writes Neil Chenoweth in *Rupert Murdoch*. 'You're talking to a butterfly mind that still manages a bewildering command of detail.'

For most business leaders, such direct engagement with media owners – from Beaverbrook more than 50 years ago to Murdoch, Michael Bloomberg or Alexander Lebedev today – carries as many risks as benefits. Disclosure of high-level media lobbying can be troublesome, raising doubts about corporate ethics, governance and sometime legal compliance. So chairmen and chief executives prefer their engagement with media owners to be discreet, often conducted through trusted intermediaries.

For much of the 1980s and 1990s, such mediation was a core service proposition for financial PR firms, many of which claimed they could manage the media.

On 14 December 1995, as a *Financial Times* reporter, I published a feature about media management tactics by PR agencies. It was headlined 'Control of the Press is the Key'. The article, prompted by a Takeover Panel investigation of alleged leaks by the PR agency Financial Dynamics, included a paragraph saying: 'According to a senior director at Brunswick – Financial Dynamics's main rival – the Panel realises that PR firms now enjoy a closer relationship with many clients than bankers and brokers. Reflecting the lack of modesty for which the industry is famed, he claimed: "For some companies, we have become their most trusted advisers – totally involved in strategic thinking about their future."'

The next day at the *FT*, my phone rang. Alan Parker, chairman and founder of Brunswick, introduced himself and said: 'You've made us sound like arseholes. I'd like to know who you spoke to at our firm.'

His call, pleasant but mildly threatening, revealed the nervousness among PR firms at media scrutiny of their activities. In the mid-1990s, and still today, most firms wanted to remain hidden from view; a barely visible part of the information chain between business and reader.

Exposure of the ties that bind financial PR firms and the media can be uncomfortable for both sides. Agencies who try too hard to influence the media, or which boast too much about such influence, look foolish when their claims become public. The media looks less competent, less objective, when its willingness to accept pre-packaged news from PR firms is similarly revealed.

To avoid such mutual discomfort, agencies and the media have cultivated a public image modelled on Church–State separation. Behind the scenes, the relationship works far more like a production line, with agencies handing on partly assembled bits of information – and sometimes near-finished news – for the media to repackage or reinterpret for public consumption.

The media, naturally, hates the idea of being part of a production line. And to prove their independence, news outlets will occasionally give a good kicking to a company or business that tries too hard to cultivate a superior reputation. The group-media tendency to negative reporting is particularly acute at times of corporate crisis, or when the media has been swept up in a market rally – only to be proved spectacularly wrong.

This is as true today as it was during the Great Crash of 1929. Before Wall Street collapsed, many New York magazines and newspapers 'reported the upward sweep of the market with admiration and awe and without alarm'.[6]

Subsequent hearings by the US Senate Committee on Banking and Currency even revealed that some reporters were being induced to ramp the market. One financial columnist on the *Daily News*, known as 'The Trader', received $19,000 from a benefactor seeking to place favourable market news.

Only the *New York Times* emerged with any credit, while other media titles seemed happy to accept frothy market sentiment. The *Times* 'was all but immune to the blandishments of the New Era,' according to J.K. Galbraith. 'To say that the *Times*, when the real crash came, reported the event with jubilation

---

[6] John Kenneth Galbraith, *The Great Crash 1929*, London, Hamish Hamilton, 1955.

would be an exaggeration. Nevertheless, it covered it with an unmistakable absence of sorrow.'

Media conduct during the Great Crash revealed the slalom pattern to relations between the media and outside interest groups, mainly PR firms and their clients. With each boom and bust, the relationship seems to swerve between mutual dependence and outright hostility. Whether at the macro level of stock market and economic reporting, or the micro coverage of particular companies, the media warms to apparent success stories – rising prices, rising profitability – and then reacts with fury at any failure or misconduct that they failed to spot.

Similar patterns of agency–media dependence and distrust preceded and then followed corporate events from the rise and fall of Polly Peck, or BCCI, to the demise of Enron.

Parts of the media hailed Enron's performance of the fraudulent energy trading business before its spectacular collapse. *Fortune* magazine named Enron 'America's most innovative company' for six consecutive years before its criminal accounting procedures were exposed.

Enron's failure signalled a new low in relations between the media and the business PR world. Journalists felt deceived and embarrassed by their inability to deliver the most accurate, incisive and timely business news. That embarrassment deepened with criticism from their own ranks. Staff at the *Financial Times*, for example, were dismayed when Marjorie Scardino, chief executive of Pearson, the information and education group behind the *FT*, criticised business journalists for failing to detect corporate wrongdoing.

'I do think the business press – and I include the *FT* in this – has not worked hard enough to ferret out these stories,' she told the *Royal Society of Arts Journal* in 2002. 'If journalists were better at reading balance sheets, some of these things would be discovered sooner. We could have done a lot more digging. But business journalists often don't know a lot about business. It's a shame, but that's the case.'

The truth was that newsrooms on both sides of the Atlantic, and beyond, were susceptible to media management in the run up to such spectacular collapses. The media swallowed the tactics of Bernie Ebbers, the disgraced former chief executive of WorldCom, who used to conduct press conferences by showing a slide of the telecom group's soar-away share price and then asking: 'Any questions?'

After each of these failures, media attitudes harden and then soften again with the next piece of adept profiling. Hence the *FT*, among others, was swept along by BP's embrace of the 'Beyond Petroleum' mantra – devoting an entire series to eulogising the work of John Browne, the oil group's chief executive. And then it caned the company over the Deepwater Horizon disaster and reported every subsequent misstep with relish.

The same was true of the sub-prime mortgage crisis and the collapse of Lehman Brothers. The media, with a few exceptions, did not predict the crisis and then bore a widely held grudge against the PR community for not somehow disclosing elements of it.

Sir Howard Stringer, chairman of Sony, is one of many corporate bosses to have felt the wrath of the business media who initially reported developments at the Japanese consumer electronics group in a glowing way, before performing a hand-brake turn, reviling the same corporate leadership for failing to live up to expectations. Widely-held media hostility to business has lingered for several years, according to Sir Howard. Diagnosing the causes, he told me in a 2010 interview: 'We're seeing a sort of journalistic backlash against the financial world.' The Sony boss felt the media's failure to detect the banking crisis had infected broader attitudes about business.

'The reality of the sub-prime mortgage crisis was that it was a bubble, and a bubble will burst, as it did with the Internet,' he said. 'Journalists want to be the ones who predict it. But journalists are also under stress at the moment. Newspapers are in trouble; advertising is in trouble; and people are worried. A *New York*

Times columnist recently called it the "pessimism bulge", which is a good way of describing the current mood.'

These mood swings between the media and the corporate world, represented by PR agencies, have caused increasing alarm among business leaders. If agencies are less able to manage the media, and the media starts out from a position of corporate hostility, how is coverage to be managed?

In recent years, the answer for many agencies has been: if you can't manage the media, you had better hire them. Over the past ten years there has been a sharp increase in the number of senior journalists crossing to the 'dark side'. With media organisations under pressure and budgets being cut, the world of public relations has proved alluring.

As a result, three former business editors of the *Sunday Times* are now working for agencies in London. The former mergers and acquisitions editor of the *Wall Street Journal* now heads up Brunswick's operation in New York. The same agency is also home to the former editor of *The Sun*, and the former banking editor of *The Independent* along with his colleague the former industry editor. The *FT* is represented there, and at rival agency Tulchan. The former business editor of the *Sunday Telegraph* now leads Maitland, another London firm. StockWell, a recently formed strategic communications provider, is led by two former *FT* staffers – myself included. Roland Rudd, the founder of Finsbury, used to sit opposite me on the UK companies desk of the *FT*. Some of our other colleagues went in-house; others went plural, acting as consultants to or writers-at-large for different corporations.

The same pattern has emerged in other major economies, including France, Germany and Spain, as well as in the financial centres of Hong Kong and New York.

The appeal of former journalists lies in their ability to anticipate the mood swings of their old colleagues. But in today's hostile environment, calling in old favours will not work, and there will be no credit given for simply sending out a press release or treating someone to lunch in the expectation of favourable coverage.

Clients and agencies hope that former journalists, at least those able to swap adversarial reporting practices for corporate advocacy, can start to repair relationships damaged by the financial crisis.

But relationships will be harder to repair if the media senses any attempt by PR firms to secure favours or to be handed news in return for a client payback at a later date.

In today's climate of public suspicion towards big business, reporters are particularly determined not to be captured by writing stories that are in the future shown to favour companies that later underperform.

John Lloyd, the *Financial Times* columnist and media commentator, highlighted this dilemma at a 2010 seminar hosted by the Reuters Institute for the Study of Journalism. In a paper to the institute, Lloyd said:

Many believe that the danger of capture is particularly high in business journalism – since, unlike political and some other reporting, journalists rely heavily on companies and financial institutions for briefings, interviews and inside knowledge. Corporations and banks, as well as governments, now employ large and skilled teams of PR specialists – often former journalists – and these are highly proactive in briefing, suggesting story lines and offering clear narratives in complex areas.

The large and rapid growth in business public relations in the past two decades and their strong influence on journalists often less well resourced than they are is seen by some journalists as alarming. On the side of the PR specialists, the view is that their interventions secure greater accuracy than would otherwise be the case.

There is no better summary of the battle-lines in media management.

It is harder for businesses and their PR agents to influence media outlets – whether titles owned once by Lord Beaverbrook or today by Rupert Murdoch. The influence of such moguls has also dissipated, proving harder to transfer from father to son. And agencies are finding, to their dismay, that it is no longer possible to manage the media simply by hiring from its ranks.

Even before the fragmenting impact of digital technology (addressed in later chapters), the old relationships of favours and information-trading between agencies and news outlets had been changing profoundly. New relationships are forming, and new methods of supply and demand are reshaping business journalism. Information has to be handled with extreme care; journalists do not want to be captive to a PR assembly line. And they are determined to prove they are not victims of spin. It is a hard lesson for the PR wizards who shaped the industry over the past 20 years. They are finding it increasingly hard to do what they once did best. They can no longer barter.

CHAPTER 4

Barter and Persuasion

A short while ago, the chairman of one of the world's largest corporations told his board he intended to stand down. Immediately, a search was instigated for a high-profile successor, someone of international experience and sufficient business stature to lead a notoriously fractious board.

Once the new chairman had been identified, and terms had been agreed, a press release was drafted by the group's head of communications. It was highly confidential, and price sensitive. Only a handful of individuals were aware of the planned board change.

About a week before the news was due to be released, the outgoing chairman persuaded the head of communications to send the draft release to the group's external PR advisers. 'I had a sinking feeling,' recalled the communications vice-president. 'Unfortunately, our chief executive was on a plane; he never would have sanctioned it.'

Once the chief executive landed, and had been informed, he raised the possibility of a damaging leak. 'There was nothing that could be done, so we placed a bet on how soon it would come out,' says the communications official. 'I predicted that the agency would plant it in the Sundays; the boss bet it would be on the front page within 24 hours. He won.'

There are persuasive arguments against leaking by PR agencies. Yet it still continues. Inside information is regularly published by the media. But much of it is not disclosed as the result of the investigative zeal of journalists. It is handed over as part of a trade, a barter, by old-style PR executives who deal in media persuasion and favours.

Client confidentiality is supposedly protected by a code of conduct in the UK, published by the Chartered Institute of

Public Relations. But it does not have regulatory force, and only urges practitioners to be 'careful to avoid using confidential and "insider" information to the disadvantage or prejudice of clients and employers, or to self-advantage of any kind'.

For many old-school PR agents, inside information is an everyday part of their communications armoury – knowledge that carries power that can be bartered. Most of these PR executives grew up in an era of few regulations and fewer sanctions, and they remain first and foremost merchants of information. Their mercantile instincts are founded on a habit of bartering. It is the basis for the negotiating style at most agencies, whether in dealings with clients or with the audiences they are seeking to influence.

Over many years as a business journalist and subsequently as PR counsel, I have been both victim of and witness to bartering. In theoretical terms, the barter-approach is derived from the principle of what psychologists call 'persuasive communications'. This defines how anyone seeking to communicate with an audience can best modify attitudes, beliefs and opinions. The ability to modify opinions – the art of persuasion – is crucial in public relations, especially when agencies are seeking to win business, negotiating fees, finding new recruits or deciding how to shape a communications campaign.

According to psychologists D.S. Wright and Ann Taylor:

Persuasive communications received its initial impetus during the [Second World] War, when there was an immediate need to devise effective techniques for maintaining morale and changing attitudes and behaviour in large numbers of people. Since then, the crucial role of mass communications in highly developed societies has confirmed and strengthened this interest.[7]

---

[7] D.S. Wright and Ann Taylor (eds.), *Introducing Psychology: An Experimental Approach*, Harmondsworth, Penguin, 1970.

The theory of persuasive communications, evolving out of war-time propaganda, is a major influence on today's financial public relations. Unlike propaganda, however, the ability to deliver business communications depends on much more than a willing messenger–audience relationship. Instead, it depends on having something to trade or barter, namely, the ability to win and retain corporate clients at one end of the value chain, or managing the positive distribution of client information at the other end of the chain – to the media.

This balancing act requires, in turn, a degree of control over three groups of variables: the first relates to the competence of the communicator; the second concerns the subject matter being communicated; the third is determined by the personality of the target audience.

In the first category, PR competence depends on what academics term 'persuasibility'. This persuasibility is influenced by factors including the communicator's prestige, their ability to deliver the intended outcome, a track record of success and some degree of affinity with the target audience – be they clients or media. If one applies that test to the leaders of PR agencies, they tend to meet these criteria. They have prestige in their industry, often as founder chairmen of successful companies. Before they start bartering in any situation, they have a fixed view of what constitutes success or failure. They are treated seriously, because they have successfully negotiated with clients and target audiences before. And in most cases they share the same attributes as the people they are dealing with.

Most client companies, for example, are run by white men or women aged between 45 and 65; as are their PR agencies. Most journalists, analysts, regulators and politicians in the world's largest capital markets are white men and women aged 30 to 60.

Hence each barter begins with a degree of familiarity.

As a journalist, it was common to get a call from Tim Bell, the chairman of Bell Pottinger and former marketing guru to Margaret Thatcher, in which he'd say 'Hello, my love' – to man or woman. Chris Blackhurst, the editor of *The Independent*, recalls getting the same treatment from Alan Parker, chairman of Brunswick. In *Management Today*, 1 February 2000, he recorded: 'He runs a fantastically successful business. His Brunswick agency seems to advise anything that moves in the FTSE-100 and much beyond. He's the multi-millionaire, not me. And he calls me boss. I know, it's all part of the appeal, of course. And I know it shouldn't make a difference, but it does.'

Lucy Kellaway, the veteran *FT* columnist, got a similar charm blast when interviewing Roland Rudd, chairman of RLM Finsbury. After noting 'the easy flattery flowing from him as smoothly as ever', she wrote in the *FT* for 12 August 2011: 'What Rudd did was to spot the way that financial PR was moving, away from the back-room activity in which fixers planted dodgy stories. Instead he (and his rival Alan Parker at Brunswick) have refashioned their trade so that they are life coaches and trusted friends to their CEO clients.'

Professional charm and prestige, along with what Kellaway calls 'the sheen of success', is vital in both securing clients and influencing the media. Hence, the Bells, Parkers and Rudds of the industry will be massively deferential to a potential client while trying to persuade them: 'We have done a lot of these sorts of deals/crises/restructuring (delete as appropriate) in the past.' To the journalist, they might add: 'I know you need another source but trust me, you won't look stupid if you write that.'

No amount of prestige and trust on the part of the communicator, however, can help if the subject being communicated is poorly presented or lacks appeal. So the second element of any negotiation, or barter, requires a clear and concise order of presentation. If the PR executive cannot explain to a journalist or another target audience why his client's position is valid, it doesn't matter how much charm or experience he or she brings to bear. Similarly, if there is no emotional appeal to their negotiating style, if right is not on your side, your communications will fall flat.

Even if these two groups of variables can be managed successfully – namely, prestige on the part of the communicator and a persuasive presentational style – the interaction with any client or external audience can founder on the third variable: the nature of the person on the receiving end.

The theory of persuasive communications, the basis of the barter system, holds that the success or failure of a pitch or communications campaign can also depend on the personality traits of the target audience linked to gender, previous experience and susceptibility to influence. Different audiences may not be swayed by communication tactics that work with others.

The chummy familiarity and false deference deployed by some UK PR leaders, for example, does not tend to play well in US corridors of power or in the formal business culture of Japan.

A suspicion of controlled leaks, of seeking media favours, also dismays corporate clients who expect PR agencies to comply with the sort of business ethics expected of other advisers. For the most part, leaks in business and financial public relations are today the exception rather than the rule. Sanctions against sharing corporate information are tougher, so leaks are less pervasive than in political lobbying. As the leader of one financial PR agency puts it: 'In politics there is always a plethora of people willing to talk on background. I suspect political journalists rely on some sources and talk to them much more than their business media counterparts. But maybe because there are more people out there talking to them on any one topic, they may end up less beholden to political sources than business ones.'

Of course, all business and financial PR leaders would deny any culture of leaking. They describe themselves as professional services practitioners, fully compliant with all regulations known to man. But there is a grey area between the theoretical elements of persuasive communications and the day-to-day allegations of leaks to favoured media outlets. This grey area is home to the barter.

Bartering is common practice because communications success is never guaranteed, even when the three core elements of persuasive communications are all in place – competent communicator, an appealing presentation and a target audience willing to believe the message.

In an attempt to guarantee better outcomes, five areas of bartering have emerged in business and financial PR. Firstly, there is the barter with clients, mostly covering the scope of support and the fees. Then there is bartering within most agencies about who handles which clients, and how the fees translate into remuneration. Thirdly, there is bartering with sources such as equity analysts, investors and non-client companies about sharing information that might be useful. The penultimate bartering skill concerns the media – haggling over the shape, tone and depth of client coverage. And lastly, there is bartering with information itself: how to derive power and influence from all sorts of data without breaching any codes of conduct.

With clients, the biggest element of the barter is focused on fees. For most agencies, retained monthly fees are paid within a fairly standard band depending on the size of the client and the intensity of the mandate. But it is broadly within a range of £5,000–15,000 for standard financial retainer work, although it can exceed ten times that figure for some mega-corporations. The real haggling starts over projects and deal fees. This is where fortunes are made, particularly serving companies in crisis.

During the course of 2010–11, crisis-hit companies were paying out several million dollars a month to PR agencies in North America and Europe which had won mandates to help them out of trouble. One agency leader jokes that: 'Unless the fee proposal induces projectile vomit, it is too low.'

In an economic downturn of corporate austerity, however, the fee barter is becoming much harder. Companies are unwilling to pay as much as they did in the past. And agencies with large overheads are finding themselves exposed to downward pressure on fees.

That pressure has intensified the internal bartering at many agencies over how people are rewarded and promoted. Each year, there is an internal wave of expectation and haggling over who is up and who is down. Executives try to barter for favours with their colleagues, seeking appraisal support that might enhance their bonuses. Others ask to be brought on to accounts that are higher profile and more remunerative.

This internal bartering over pay and conditions is matched, for intensity, by an external barter for useful information from sources such as equity analysts and institutional investors. Clients will pay more, it is assumed, for client handlers who have useful industry intelligence about changing market conditions and industrial trends. PR executives set a premium on such information, which they will barter from various sources in exchange for hospitality, for client introductions or for access to their broader business networks.

The media is the fourth and arguably most intensive focus for bartering. This is where the theory of persuasive communications is put into practice. In most developed economies, the business media is thought to be persuadable. Agencies know that the media is itself under threat. Reporters are desperate for information or news that can enhance their coverage. PR agencies have something the media want: access and information.

Given the pressures on newsgathering, promises from PR agencies of both access and information have become increasingly important for news outlets. Research conducted at Cardiff University's school of journalism, commissioned by *Guardian* journalist Nick Davies, found that more than 40 per cent of UK news stories in Britain's five most prestigious newspapers 'were initiated by PR and/or contained material supplied by PR, and a further 13 per cent of stories carried clear signs of PR activity, but the researchers were unable finally to prove the point, because the PR trail was too well hidden, usually through off-the-record briefings.'[8]

Similarly, a study of the *Wall Street Journal* by the *Columbia Journalism Review*, also cited by Davies, found that 'more than half of the news stories "were based solely on press releases" ... with little additional reporting but with the classic and dishonest byline "By a *Wall Street Journal* staff reporter".'

Such reports, and similar claims about PR influence in other leading economies, would suggest that the barter system is working well – at least in terms of agency ability to extend client interests. But that explanation is too simplistic and fails to acknowledge the often adversarial nature of the way information is bartered between agencies and the media.

This is the fifth bartering discipline, directly affecting how information gets to market.

The world's business media are not yet so pliable that they accept PR briefing at face value. Indeed, there has been a rise in what John Lloyd, the *Financial Times* commentator, calls 'laser-guided journalism'. It strikes fear into the hearts of corporations and their PR agencies.

However persuasive and prestigious the PR firm, their ability to barter with information on favourable terms with the media has been undermined in recent years by a change in media sentiment towards outright hostility to the business world. 'Laser-guided journalism goes straight to what it conceives of as the heart of darkness and remains there, demanding an explanation for the darkness on its own terms,' writes Lloyd. 'The relative weight of what is seen as the heart of darkness is not its business: by shining its laser-guided beam on it, [the media] elevates it to an absolute importance.'[9]

This changing balance in communications supply and demand, with different PR suppliers all bartering for favourable

---

[8] Nick Davies, *Flat Earth News*, London, Vintage, 2009.
[9] John Lloyd, *What the Media are Doing to Our Politics*, London, Constable, 2004.

coverage from a hostile media pack demanding explanations, has begun to challenge the powers of persuasion claimed by many agencies.

Even if they put in place all the elements required to be persuasive communicators, and even if they can be trusted to handle information with care, PR executives at such agencies are today finding it harder to barter on terms that clients will pay for.

CHAPTER 5

Battle for Scoops

In today's aggressive, digital and ultra-competitive news environment, few business reporters have time for proverbs. But there is one they would probably all subscribe to: 'Lucky men need no counsel.'[10]

For no amount of PR counselling, no amount of rehearsal and preparation can prevent business stories that have been secured by sheer luck or guile. Yet a whole industry of financial PR has grown up with the purpose of taking lucky scoops out of the news equation. Under the media management skills claimed by many PR companies, significant emphasis is often given to the ability to control messaging, to prevent unsanitised or unplanned information reaching external audiences.

This 'prepare and protect' approach to corporate information, adopted by most traditional PR companies, creates a natural tension with business journalists whose purpose is to shine a light on business news that some companies would prefer to keep under wraps. This tension has increased in recent years, given the pressure on reporters to deliver scoops to the front page or to camera.

The competitive tension between news organisations has increased as they each pursue exclusives in an attempt to reassert their relevance to audiences faced with an unprecedented choice of sources of information. This tension has escalated in the digital age, especially in the desperate battle between analogue media brands and digital 'citizen journalists' to break revelatory news and gossip.

Companies and their PR agencies often feel caught in the cross-fire between news organisations seeking to out-scoop each other. Business leaders are particularly alarmed by high profile

---

[10] H.G. Bohn, *A Handbook of Proverbs*, London, H.G. Bohn, 1855.

correspondents who see themselves as owners of corporate stories, prompting them to begin each report or blog post with the self-congratulatory phrases: 'I can exclusively reveal' or 'For the first time, we have learned that' or 'As I first reported'.

The fight for exclusives, long a staple diet of tabloid journalism (with spectacularly devastating effects of industrial-scale phone-hacking in Britain), is also increasingly important for serious business titles. As Robert Thompson, editor in chief of *Dow Jones* and managing editor of the *Wall Street Journal*, said in the *Brunswick Review* of winter 2011: 'If someone breaks a lot of stories, is good on the web, and articulate when forced to explain something in 30 seconds before a camera, clearly that woman or man has a very bright future in journalism.'

In today's digital environment, particularly for breaking business news, 30 seconds is a lifetime. Scoops in a digital environment are not just about reliability; they are about speed. So traditional wire agencies such as Reuters and Bloomberg have invested heavily in automated systems that can 'read' a news release and flash the headlines to financial trading rooms in nanoseconds.

The chief executive of one agency explains the need for speed, saying: 'Any latency [time lag] costs money. It has been estimated that cutting latency by one millisecond – one thousandth of a second – can be worth $100 million dollars to a big trading house. The old adage, taken from the world of sports, that first is first and second is nowhere, has never been truer.'

As a result, genuine exclusives command a value premium. Wire agencies measure the time taken for reporters to get stories on to trading screens, with embarrassing post-mortems for anyone deemed too slow. Reuters, part of Thomson Reuters, has even invested in computerised systems in Bangalore, India that can convert a digital news release into an instant story and flash it to the world far faster than any human reporter.

In this world, companies and their PR agencies set even greater store on controlling the flow of information.

But when real scoops emerge, they are often as much by luck as judgment on the part of the journalists involved. I know. I was a lucky journalist. Lucky journalists are the bane of PR firms, and their clients. They can detonate well-laid plans and shorten the careers of PR executives who fail to see the impending news revelation.

Of course, journalists make their own luck. Part of the job is to cultivate contacts and seek background briefings that might result in an unguarded aside or off-the-record quote that creates a major news story. But engaging on those terms is central to the work of public relations; what is unmanageable is where the journalist stumbles into a situation by chance, and where no amount of spin control can rescue the client.

These unmanageable scoops are often down to PR failures; the industry's equivalent of pilot error. And they certainly pre-date the digital era, as I witnessed.

In November 1996, as a *Financial Times* journalist, I tele-phoned Shandwick, then an influential financial PR firm. I needed to check some facts about T&N, the UK engineering group locked in a long-running campaign to cap its asbestos liabilities. But the switchboard at the agency put me straight on to a conference call about an imminent and secret M&A trans-action. Should I hang up or press mute? Like any ambitious business journalist of the time, I pressed mute. For the next 20 minutes, I listened with awe to the discussion between clients, bankers and PR executives. After a polite interlude at the end of the call, I called Shandwick again and asked to speak to the PR executives representing the company in question. They were aghast at the *FT*'s 'discovery', which made the next day's front page. Was it subterfuge or illegal eavesdropping? There was no intent. For the journalist, it was a lucky break; for the PR agency, it was a calamity.

Accidental scoops are frequently down to basic technical errors, such as the Shandwick telephone operator misdirect-ing my call. Similarly, it was cock-up, not conspiracy, when the

London agency representing Tie Rack, the ubiquitous neck-wear company, sent out to the media not the company's earnings press release but the biographies of all the journalists due to meet the company, leading to all sorts of revelations about whom Tie Rack should fear and whom it should cosset.

Technical errors are sometimes compounded by agencies and clients failing to spot a new journalist on the beat. Most news organisations move correspondents between industrial beats every three to four years, an exercise that refreshes the coverage and prevents any reporter from being captured by an industry – or 'going native'. The newly arrived beat reporter, anxious to prove his or her mettle, has about two months in which they are an unknown quantity to clients and agencies.

This is a prime time in which they can stumble upon all sorts of accidental information, and they have been known to cause internal recriminations at the companies affected. In 1999, the German industrial powerhouse of Daimler Benz had merged with the US carmaker Chrysler. The two companies were determined to make a splash at that year's Frankfurt auto show, their first public outing as the newly formed DaimlerChrysler. Generously, Daimler had offered the incoming *FT* motor industry correspondent one of their block-booked hotel rooms in Frankfurt after the *FT* failed to secure anywhere to stay.

In the hotel room, made available by a DaimlerChrysler executive's late cancellation, there was a helpful invitation to a pre-show briefing – which the *FT* correspondent duly attended. About 20 minutes into the meeting, at which DaimlerChrysler officials were discussing various coming announcements including a $60 billion investment in new products, the reporter realised it was not a press briefing at all. It was a management meeting for what was about to be revealed in the coming days. All the Daimler executives in the room, meeting their US counterparts for the first time, assumed the *FT* man was from Chrysler. The team from Michigan assumed he was from Daimler. The story made the front page.

It is hard for companies and their PR firms to argue that such accidents, compounded by journalistic good fortune, amount to subterfuge. It is not a breach of any sort of code to take advantage of companies failing to make the proper checks on who attends their meetings, or indeed to check who might be sitting next to their chief executives.

In July 2002, the newly appointed media editor of the *Financial Times* was dispatched to the annual gathering of media moguls in Sun Valley, Idaho that was organised by Allen & Co., the US investment bank. The media were not admitted to the conference, where delegates ranged from Michael Eisner, then chairman and chief executive of Walt Disney, to Bill Gates of Microsoft and Rupert Murdoch of News Corp. But there were no rules against sitting near the moguls as they chatted about the industry or forthcoming deals. Each morning, at about 7am, the News Corp chairman would shamble on to the terrace of the resort's alpine lodge.

Even back then, Mr Murdoch was a little hard of hearing. So he used to shout into his mobile phone. He had never clapped eyes on the *FT*'s new media editor before, so he carried on with his call from the neighbouring table. The call was clearly long distance, as Rupert shouted: 'Our numbers are there. We are not moving an inch and we want absolute openness about this – where are you? Paris or Rome?' The master of the media universe then proceeded with deal talk about the forthcoming planned creation of Sky Italia, a transaction that would make News Corp the only pay-TV rival to Silvio Berlusconi's Mediaset.

At Sun Valley, such moguls often drop their guard and make off-the-cuff comments that strike fear into their media handlers. Hence John Malone, the normally taciturn chairman of the Liberty Media cable empire, told a small cluster of reporters: 'Corporate America is in the mix-master.' He added that recent corporate scandals and market nervousness 'looks to me like spring – when the snow melts and you see the dog shit that's been there all winter.' Both Murdoch's and Malone's comments were reported in the *FT* on 16 July 2002.

For the most part, heads of corporate communications at groups such as Liberty Media or News Corp just shrug their shoulders at such accidental story gifts. It is part of the game. Some days the journalists win, finding out a titbit of information; sometimes they lose, failing to ask – to your incredulity as an adviser – the obvious question. This is all part of the chase, the back and forth in a relationship of mutual dependence.

But sometimes it is serious, literally a matter of life and death. It is then that the spin machine goes into full drive, fed by media managers hoping to control a certain outcome. Such activist media management is growing in business public relations, taking its lead from the tactics of government spin-doctors.

Such spin and counter-spin is a daily part of political discourse in most developed markets. But in Britain, it probably reached its zenith in the summer of 2003, when a full-blown war of words erupted between the British government and the BBC over Iraq's alleged weapons of mass destruction. The entire political press corps and much of the media beat were seeking the identity of the source who told Andrew Gilligan, then a reporter for Radio 4's *Today* programme, that intelligence information was included in a dossier on weapons of mass destruction at the behest of Downing Street and against the wishes of the intelligence community. As reported in the *FT* on 10 July, Gilligan quoted the official as saying that the 'classic example of this' was the suggestion that Iraq could fire chemical and biological weapons within 45 minutes of giving an order.

At the time, I was media editor of the *FT*, and the BBC was a central part of the beat. My then colleague, *FT* political editor James Blitz, called one day in July 2003, saying he understood that Gilligan's source was David Kelly, a senior adviser in the proliferation and arms control secretariat at the Ministry of Defence. We needed to establish from the BBC whether he was their source, or if in the absence of confirmation whether they would deny it. My contacts declined to deny it. We reported their position as: 'The BBC refused to say last night whether Mr Kelly was the single source of the story.'

Within a fortnight, Dr Kelly was dead and, as reported on 22 July in the *FT*, it emerged that Geoff Hoon, then defence secretary, had personally authorised his department's strategy for dealing with the scientist. The *FT* had been merely the first, and quite an unlikely outlet, to get David Kelly's name and to secure a non-denial from the BBC. It was an exclusive that no one celebrated and which ended with tragic consequences.

Ultimately, the affair led to the resignations of both Gavyn Davies, chairman of the BBC board of governors, and the corporation's director general Greg Dyke. Before Davies quit, and before the government-appointed Hutton inquiry delivered a damning verdict on BBC conduct, I got a call early one morning from Tim Allan, founder of the public affairs agency Portland and a former deputy press secretary at Downing Street for Tony Blair. 'You'd better get a lawyer,' he said. 'Your name has come up in the Hutton inquiry.'

The call from Allan, who relished the discomfort of the BBC, was prompted by a report in *The Guardian*, on 8 September, which said: 'Fresh evidence published on the Hutton inquiry website today revealed that the BBC chairman, Gavyn Davies, had been briefing the *Financial Times* media editor, Tim Burt, off the record in the days following Dr Kelly's death.'

In the event, I was deemed small fry, not worthy of further inquiry. Lord Hutton had far bigger issues to deal with.

The whole affair, in which Dr Kelly's conduct and the reporting standards of the BBC were made the story, revealed the extent to which demand for scoops or the search for exclusives could have outcomes that no one imagined. The reporters on the story were all persuaded that it was about the dangerous lapse in checks and balances at the world's leading publicly funded broadcaster, and not about the substance of the government's claims about Iraq's weapons of mass destruction.

Ultimately, the substance of the BBC's report was shown to be true, if not the manner in which it reported it. Since then, the scoop-driven culture of twenty-first-century media, which lay at the root of Andrew Gilligan's controversial story about the government's claims of Iraq's weapons capability, has encouraged a cadre of journalists – covering business and other sectors – who are ready to take major risks with stories.

Those dangers exploded in 2011–12 with the revelations of the phone-hacking culture at the *News of the World*, the flagship Sunday tabloid of News International, the UK publishing arm of News Corp. Throughout, News International has argued that illegal hacking was confined to rogue reporters at its Sunday title, which was shut down in the summer of 2011.

But back in 2003, in the same month that David Kelly was exposed in the weapons controversy, an adjudication was issued by the Press Complaints Commission (PCC) – apparently overlooked in subsequent events. In it, the PCC chastised *The Sun*, the *News of the World*'s sister paper, for publishing transcripts of telephone conversations involving the property developer linked to the 'Cheriegate' saga, in which Tony Blair's wife was accused of misleading officials about apartments purchased in Bristol.

'Eavesdropping into private telephone conversations – and then publishing transcripts of them – is one of the most serious forms of physical intrusion into privacy,' said the PCC in its ruling, reported in the *FT* on 2 July 2003. It is hard to imagine how those conversations could be made public without somebody hacking into the phones of those involved. Such conduct – magnified by the phone-hacking scandal – has spread alarm among PR agencies hired to promote and protect the reputations of individuals and corporations in the public eye.

For the most part, business leaders are relieved that the focus of the scoop culture pervading UK and US journalism has been on 'front half' stories – away from the business pages. But they are far from complacent, and far from reassured.

The continued media imperative on exclusives – scoops at any price, obtained controversially or by accident – is starting to force a full-blown reassessment of how to deal with reporters ready to take risks.

CHAPTER 6

Return on Investment

Since the great recession of 2008, the twin pressures of a media swing to scoop journalism and general business uncertainty have persuaded many corporations to reassess the value for money from financial public relations.

Large companies are bound to question the relevance and return on investment from outside PR agencies in a business climate where the media is harder to manage and where reporters are chasing exclusives – often at the expense of accuracy. As a result, agency budgets have been under pressure for several years. Tight restraints on advisory spending have been relaxed only for moments of extreme crisis or to handle major transactions.

The age of austerity has been marked by downward pressure on fees, with some companies building year-on-year reductions into their contracts. Others have dispensed with outside advisers altogether. One leading FTSE-100 company, one of the largest global players in its sector, recently told its long-term agency that if it wished to retain the account, it would have to accept a 50 per cent haircut on the monthly fee. Another corporation, a household name in the USA, insisted that its PR advisers should sign the same procurement terms and conditions as it demanded from suppliers of sanitary equipment and catering services, all of whom were expected to deliver annualised savings of 12 per cent.

'There is a secular trend to lower retained fees,' says the head of corporate communications at one of Britain's top 20 companies. 'Budgets are being reallocated to advertising and promotion. So we are re-examining all fees that do not help move product, including legal advice, management consultancy and non-audit work.'

For many agencies, the decline in average client retainers might have been tolerable, had there been a compensating wave of mergers and acquisitions commanding large project fees, often with a success element attached. But M&A has been in relatively short supply in recent years, compounding the fee pressure.

The absence of deal income has been offset, for a lucky few firms, by a series of corporate crises in which troubled businesses – some of them in panic – have handsomely rewarded agencies that promised 'a get out of jail' service. But such payments, reaching $3 million a month for one agency handling a recent major crisis, are the exception rather than the rule. Agencies have tried to put a brave face on the situation. 'Crisis is the new M&A' is the optimistic refrain repeated by some client handlers. But the frequency of such crises and the fees accompanying them are less predictable, and often less generous than deal mandates.

The squeeze on fees has been particularly uncomfortable for larger agencies with significant cost overheads, mostly people. They staffed up during the good times; now they need to slim. Hence, the latest downturn has been the PR industry's equivalent of an enforced gastric band: the hunger is still there; you have an appetite. But you have no choice but to lose weight.

The weight-loss programme means shedding the heaviest cost. For an agency, this usually means cutting the number of partners or managing directors, particularly those who struggle to retain clients or whose remuneration package might exceed the combined salaries of several talented, junior and ambitious young executives.

Of course, there have been heavy cost-cutting and periods of cyclical decline before. The hiring and firing mood swing has been a feature of the sector for years. Ten years ago, there was a severe squeeze on fees and margins following a near 40 per cent decline in mergers and acquisitions mandates. Hundreds of jobs were axed. Fee income was shredded for some firms. Others, who had listed on the stock market, saw their stock plummet. As the downturn began to bite in the first two years of the twenty-first century, Chime plc – one of the few listed PR firms – was typical of the price that was paid. It saw its share price fall from 200p to 14p.

'The long boom of the late 1990s saw lavish PR spending as deal after deal had to be explained, advocated, sold,' according to the article in the *New Statesman* for 20 January 2003 by Stefan Stern, the management writer who later went into public relations. 'PR firms were compared to businesses such as McKinsey or Goldman Sachs. Their staff were likened to sophisticated management consultants or capital market geniuses. Their fees rose accordingly.'

His warning, issued during the last industry recession, resonates today. 'While today an elite core of PR experts continues to provide important and valuable communications advice to their clients – the business world hasn't stopped breathing altogether – for many travelling PR men and women, the bubble has burst.'

What is so far unclear is whether the bubble will reflate. There are fears in parts of the industry that financial PR agencies are experiencing a structural threat to their model; this is not the normal supply-and-demand cycle. 'The edict has gone out from the chief financial officer: no more consultancies,' says the corporate affairs director at one FTSE-100 company. 'And if we have to utilise agencies, it has to be a very small team with strategic insight. It's not about throwing a protective cloak around the chairman and chief executive.'

Such austerity measures stand in sharp contrast to the 'go-go' years of financial communications.

Fee inflation was a natural expectation in the golden decades between the 'Big Bang' of 1986 – when market deregulation finally reached the City of London – and the collapse of Lehman Brothers in 2008. For most of that period, external PR advisers were regarded by companies of all shapes and sizes as a vital and justifiable expense. Under the accepted business case of the time, the media and other audiences had to be managed. Companies and their advisers had a job of persuasion to do. Audiences needed to be told why corporate strategies were right, and why their management was the best. Money was thrown around liberally.

The strategic communications plan of one large US industrial group demonstrates the budgets available in the pre-Lehman era. Citing the need to strengthen its image and reputation, the company's in-house PR team sought approval to increase total communications spending from $65.2 million a year to more than $90 million.

According to the group's budget submission: 'We aim to strengthen our impact and reputation by focusing on the quality of management and people – the "bench"; the quality of products and services – a philosophy of "disciplined pizzazz"; our improving financial condition; and innovation demonstrated by a history of "firsts".'

In seeking a 38 per cent budget increase, the communications team of this particular company promised to 'use our strengths to realize opportunities, minimize weaknesses and eliminate threats'. In what was called 'the budget walk', the corporation's treasury department was asked to support a range of global image events costing more than a million dollars; another million dollars for an 'innovation symposium'; along with a $700,000 spend on its media website; more than $900,000 for the corporate museum and $300,000 to measure media sentiment – hopefully enhanced by all this largesse. When this plan was put to the group's seven-member executive committee, there was unanimous support for most of the measures.

But a few hundred thousand here and there amounted to a rounding error compared with the big ticket item of a corporate communications budget: product public relations. In the case of this US corporation, a US household name, more than $50 million of its proposed $90 million PR budget was earmarked for product communications in its home market.

The figure did not include any sums for advertising, sales or marketing promotion. That was subject to another budget, guarded jealously by the chief marketing officer, which was considerably larger.

The product PR investment was targeted at media activity and profile-raising for the company's flagship models, including new launches, image events, industry shows and sports-related product placement. Of the rest of the communications budget, $14 million was proposed for international promotions; another $4 million for engineering, technology and design communications; almost $10 million for internal communications; and $4 million for safety communications. That left $5.5 million for corporate communications, of which the executive committee decided to ring-fence half for diversity messaging. Financial PR firms around the world were left to fight for a share of the remainder.

This budget split broadly reflects the division of fees across the PR industry as a whole. The lion's share of spending is devoted to product communications, targeted principally at a company's dominant home market. The next-largest and fast-growing segment is international product communications, followed by internal spending and then – depending on the market segment – by further allocations for technology, design, legal and diversity communications.

Product communications remains the target of lavish communications spending because there is often a visible payback, in terms of positive media coverage. If a travel company hosts a group of journalists on a junket, there is an unwritten contract that reviews will follow.

Spending on corporate and financial communications is harder to justify because the outcome might be no coverage at all, with success defined as keeping the client out of the spotlight.

By comparison, the organisation and spending on product PR is staggering, making some of the events organised by financial agencies look paltry. Car launches are good examples of the campaign planning and investment lavished on consumer media in the expectation of glossy reviews. One leading manufacturer, launching a flagship model, took over Skibo Castle in northern Scotland for six weeks to host visiting motoring correspondents. The lucky journalists, flown business class from around the world, made the last leg of the journey in a chartered passenger aircraft that had been repainted with the carmaker's logo. Before arriving at Skibo, the fleet of new vehicles – each with a reporter at the wheel – drove to a picturesque loch, where the manufacturer had paid for a temporary café on a floating pontoon. Tea and cakes were served on the water, enabling the media to enjoy the 'room with a view'. Dinners and entertainment were to follow. Not satisfied, some of the journalists on the 'Russian rotation' stole the DVD players from the Skibo bedrooms before returning home.

Another manufacturer flew groups of journalists to Venice, a city not really suited to 'ride and drive' motoring tests. The visit was organised as a gallery tour, with new cars artfully displayed alongside more valuable works. In the hotel room of every reporter, the host company deposited a heavyweight artbook as a keepsake. Sadly, the card explaining the complimentary gift was misplaced in one room. Only at check-out, with the journalist wheeling a large TV-set through reception, did the PR team realise their mistake.

A short while later, another global manufacturer hired a palazzo near Lake Garda to host a weekend seminar for business media and equity analysts. It chartered a giant transport aircraft to bring one model of every vehicle in its range, from around the world, to Italy. The cost of the three-day event was about $8 million.

Such investment is harder to justify in the second decade of the twenty-first century. But the 'gift and take' of consumer public relations still continues. Companies in consumer electronics, in aerospace, pharmaceuticals, automotive and leisure industries continue to spend heavily on launch events. As one company puts it: 'We must create and implement PR initiatives to continue the drumbeat of new products, including after they have arrived in dealer showrooms.'

Yet even this area is not immune to cutbacks. More and more companies are taking such product communications and launch events in-house, depriving consumer agencies of much needed income. One leading agency recently laid off more than 70 staff, removing an entire floor of its headquarters, after losing a consumer product account worth £15 million a year.

Even before the financial crisis of 2008, the budgets available for such product communications were coming under greater client scrutiny; and heavy cuts were being implemented in the business and financial end of the PR market.

For many years, the one exception – the one bright spot – was mergers and acquisitions. Public relations firms, during the heady days of the takeover boom, modelled their fee structures on those of investment banks. 'M&A advisers routinely contracted for a small, flat retainer fee plus a percentage of any future transaction involving their client,' wrote Steve Coll in the *Washington Post* in 1982, describing the 1980s battle for Getty Oil. 'The bigger the client, then, the more expensive was the transaction and the higher the potential fee.'

Some firms continue to command significant fees on deals, which have not evaporated altogether. Brunswick, one of the largest financial PR firms, worked on more than 180 transactions in 2011, worth a total of almost $240 billion. FTI Consulting, one of Brunswick's arch rivals, led the industry in terms of the number of deal mandates, working on 235 transactions. The numbers look rich, and some fees are. But agency insiders admit that the overall industry trend is downward, no matter the size of the deals or the volumes.

Certainly, the finance directors of large companies are less tolerant of egregious fee proposals for defence mandates. Sky-high fees might have been tolerated in the past on the unspoken understanding that the bidding company would end up paying the tab. Not any more. In one instance, involving a multi-billion euro German transaction, a leading local agency proposed a €1 million fee only to be told by the finance director of the client company: 'You must be crazy. I will pay €100,000 with no success element, and you have five minutes to take it or get out.'

In another German transaction, code-named Project Mozart, an agency asked a leading Bavarian company for €11 million to handle a high profile takeover battle. The agency was thrown out of the process, only to accept a lower fee advising investors on the other side of the deal.

The ability of firms to propose such fees takes chutzpah in the first place. And some fee proposals are plain reckless, putting long-term relationships under tremendous pressure. In today's tougher business climate, the 'open season' of huge payouts on deals is probably coming to a close, with all advisers having to justify their costs in a more quantifiable way. Such costs are expected to come under even more scrutiny because of new disclosure rules on advisory fees, introduced in 2011 among several amendments to the UK Takeover Code.

The additional scrutiny is coinciding with pressure on retainers. As in-house capabilities mature and become more sophisticated, the willingness to pay generously for additional agency support is declining. Where support is required, corporate affairs directors are demanding strategic counsel, not tactical hand-to-hand combat with the media. And they demand deep industry knowledge, rather than the ability to persuade a friendly journalist to pull a story.

That trend has accelerated since the last cyclical downturn in deal activity. Many clients are now looking for different levels of support, rather than hiring legacy PR brands because of the campaign medals they may have earned in previous deal battles.

'If you rely for fees from corporates, from deal flows and mergers and acquisitions then, to put it politely, you are fucked. Consumer PR is more than holding up,' said Matthew Freud, founder of the agency that carries his name, speaking to the

Daily Telegraph on 25 August 2002 during the last downturn. Forecasting the model that is gaining ground today, he added: 'Good PR is about small companies working hard for their clients who are looking for value.'

The search for value is not only about lower fees. It is about securing PR support that involves genuine results. That, in turn, has exacerbated the frustration felt by clients who need to see a tangible return on investment.

In an era of fewer deals and unpredictable crisis projects, a business model founded on the promise of favourable coverage is going through a painful readjustment. For public relations, it is not yet a full-blown industrial revolution. But change is coming. Business and financial PR firms are just hoping it will arrive slowly, giving them time to alter their service offering. They know the challenge ahead. Clients are impatient for services where delivery matches the promise. Professionalism is in; the old party atmosphere is over.

CHAPTER 7

Rules of the Club

Almost every Monday, the head of one of London's leading financial PR firms hosts a lunch for senior industrialists and opinion formers at the Garrick Club, in the city's theatre district.

The private gathering aims to comply with the founding principles of the Garrick, established in 1831 so that 'actors and men of refinement and education might meet on equal terms' and to facilitate 'easy intercourse ... between artists and patrons'.

The PR artist in this case promises to enhance the diners' social and business connections; the patrons are the corporate leaders who might deliver client work in future.

Around the table, more than 180 years after the Garrick first opened its doors, you might find businessmen such as Jim Leng, a non-executive director of Alstom, Sir Michael Peat, the former private secretary to the Prince of Wales, or Sir John Rose, former chief executive of Rolls-Royce. Across town, the head of another PR firm is usually to be found hosting a similar gathering at Claridge's; another favours the Savoy. Across the Atlantic, their US counterparts can be found dining their contacts at the Core Club, on East 55th Street. In Hong Kong, the industry converges on Lupa and Alfie's. For breakfasts in London, it's the Wolseley on Piccadilly where the industry breaks bread; in New York, it's Michael's in mid-town.

The diners in the respective cities are all members of a club vital to commerce: the club of business elites. And these clubs – networks of influential business leaders – are a hunting ground for the world's PR predators.

Over the years, the financial and business PR industry has managed to disguise the predatory pursuit of business contacts in a form of hospitality. The PR-dietary schedule – breakfast, lunch and dinner – are pivotal moments in the working day, when existing and potential clients are wined and dined for business.

The culinary engagement is just one part of an elaborate set of club rules that have governed traditional agencies for years. Other rules govern disclosure, recruitment, media planning and client entertainment. When it comes to hospitality, detailed records are kept of which contacts prefer certain types of entertainment; who was taken to Ascot last year; who came to the box at the test match – £6,000 for the day – or joined your party at Wimbledon (£10,000); or who attended the preview evening at Chelsea Flower Show.

In the years before the Lehman collapse, and the ensuing budget retrenchment, dinner for two at Wiltons on Jermyn Street might set the firm back £700 (plus cigars), with a cheery wave from the departing PR executive that he would be back tomorrow. The restaurant culture is so ingrained that the industry magazine *PR Week* runs a regular column – 'Saving on Expenses' – where different advisers report on the 'signature dishes' and 'the damage' charged by different eateries.

To the disquiet of some client companies, they found they were being charged to dine with their own PR consultants. To add insult to injury, their advisers charged a 20 per cent mark up on the bill they subsequently received. Such day-to-day charging – some say gouging – of clients is widely accepted within the industry as a cost of doing business. And most clients continue to pay up, unable to prove that their performance and strategy was not the subject of a media dinner.

But such costs pale against what the PR industry spends on entertaining itself. Take over a large part of Blenheim Palace for the weekend; why not? Let's fly everyone in the partnership to New York or Beijing or Washington DC for a long weekend. A banquet on the River Seine, with floating band on board? No problem. Dinner for 200 at the Natural History Museum with Abba tribute band after the petits fours? You got it. One firm decided to celebrate an anniversary by hiring horse-drawn carriages for its entire staff to go to dinner. Another took over a large part of Chewton Glen, the five-star country house hotel in southern England, only to be told never to come back after naked antics on the front lawn.

PR firms rationalise such expenditure by claiming they have to bond with staff, and to celebrate the shared success in bumper fee years. But given the choice, most staff would probably rather have a coffee and croissant with their bosses, a chance to moan a bit and a couple of thousand pounds in their backpocket instead of participating in the forced jollity.

The age of austerity in financial public relations has not been restricted to downward pressure on fees. Greater compliance, tougher procurement negotiations and a fear of media disclosure have all combined to rein in the excesses of the PR 'club'. But in many agencies and in many global financial centres, the club rules are still applied – based on the assumption that business elites are all part of some grand networking machine.

There is a widely held view in traditional PR agencies – or 'shops' as their founders like to call them – that new business flows from who you know, rather than what you know. And to secure access to the elite decision-makers, it means being part of their 'club'.

In London, Roland Rudd, the former *FT* journalist and founder of Finsbury, represents the zenith of the club approach to communications. In the *Financial Times* of 12 August 2011, Lucy Kellaway, Rudd's former *FT* colleague and an acute essayist of corporate ego, asked the Finsbury founder how the club worked:

> Just supposing, I ask, I was interested in building up my own network like Rudd's. How would I begin? Easy, he says. Simply ring up some big names in different areas and invite them over for an excellent dinner. But what if I didn't know them? 'They'd come,' he says confidently.
>
> Thus, once a fortnight, Rudd assembles an assortment of famous guests at his vast house in Holland Park

around a table that seats 18. Halfway through dinner, he hits fork against glass and insists they discuss the themes that Rudd loves – the wonders of the European Union, or the alternative vote … 'It's great fun,' he insists.

Similar dinners are thrown by agency leaders in the world's largest capital markets. And the club also goes on tour: to Davos for the World Economic Forum annual meeting in January, to the Aspen Institute's 'Ideas Festival' in June, to the Allen & Co. media and technology summit at Sun Valley in July, or the Monaco media conference hosted by Publicis, the French marketing services group, in September. Members of the club might convene in Corfu in August, often clustering around the Rothschild family villas; or in Cape Town for mid-winter.

At such locations, traditional PR leaders tend to gravitate to the rich and powerful in industry like moths around a light. Whenever they can, they are selling their agency wares, comparing themselves to the trusted advisers – the investment banker and management consultants – that have created lucrative fee-based businesses which members of the PR club regard with envious eyes.

Admission to the club of business elites is seen as a mark of approval by PR leaders – something they aspire to and model themselves on. Chris Blackhurst, the editor of *The Independent*, detected the club-envy more than a decade ago when he interviewed Alan Parker, the founder and chairman of Brunswick.

Recording his meeting with Parker in the business magazine *Management Today*, 1 February 2000, Blackhurst wrote:

He stops jumping around to talk seriously, and passionately, about having Brunswick emulate his business heroes, whom he names as McKinsey, Lazards, Cazenove and Goldman Sachs. Even for someone who specialises in the art of spin, that is not a bad list. There is, though, a deliberate purpose behind his boast. Method, if you like, in his apparent madness. Their names are bywords for professional service and discretion. They are all global and unquestionably at the pinnacle of their industries … All four, in a Parker word, are 'class'.

The quest for lustre, for stature above the run of the mill, is a theme to which Parker warms, likening his model for the development of Brunswick to that of a prestigious law firm. Financial PR is 'a serious business, not a bullshit business for one-offs. Communicating properly is a proper business, not a scam, not a fix.'

The old club nature of the financial PR world is a double-edged sword. It has opened doors to business secured by personal favours: the old system of feudal patronage. But it has also slowed down attempts to secure business legitimacy. The relentless networking, the aversion to outside scrutiny, the appetite for parties and the dinner-table pursuit of clients has hindered attempts by some agencies to be recognised as professional services organisations.

Yet in an industry with limited regulation and few fully transparent firms, the self-imposed rules of the club still carry weight.

Those rules include the principle that your firm should, at all costs, only ever be the intermediary in a company's story – never the story itself. That is always a hard bargain to make when so many firms heavily sell the idea that they can manage the media. The media occasionally delights in exposing the absurdity of some PR activity, especially the vain attempts to blunt negative coverage of a prized client. But if you engage with the media, you should be prepared to fall under its spotlight; there is always a risk that the agency will become the story rather than the messenger.

In spite of occasional unwelcome coverage, one of the golden rules of financial PR remains to be 'heard but not seen' in the media. Other club rules include absolute discretion when it comes to client confidentiality; always prioritising vulnerable relationships and treating your colleagues as vital components of a single machine.

One leading agency chairman recently told his global partners:

> There are a few basic rules we must observe. We must try to create a genuinely networked firm. Everyone is a cog in that engine. But if we play it right, we could grow significantly because we're all just scratching the surface. What we're capable of doing is significantly greater. We have to grow our sub-scale offices; we must be a multidisciplinary shop with genuine capabilities in not just financial communications but in public affairs, in regulatory work and in crisis projects. Those are things that will make this club, this community, really work.

The club rules that apply within the agency world apply also to the broad ecosystem in which agencies operate. Just as PR firms try to play by an unwritten set of regulations, in which each firm competes hard for business but generally respects the others, so they also operate a set of rules, a code of common behaviour, in dealing with other stakeholders. Of those stakeholders, some generate business, notably investment bankers and law firms. Others consume business, taking time and effort to manage – of which the most demanding group is, of course, the media.

Some PR agency leaders regard the media as a vast club, subdivided into different membership groups comprising the print pack, the broadcasting pack, the freelance pack, a commentary pack and, more recently, the online pack. In each of these areas, the journalistic community is clustered around particular beats such as banking, economics, consumer industries, defence, retail and so on. This is a huge convenience for PR firms and their clients, who can use the beat system to target relatively small audiences at outlets where the senior editorial team are often hard to reach or hard to influence.

Nowhere is this system more formalised than in Japan, where American post-war administrators created press clubs for different industries, for politics, economics and for individual companies to ensure that the media received fair and equal access to news. Although the club system has been challenged by the arrival of digital media, it remains a powerful mechanism for corporate disclosure.

Club rules are less rigorously applied in other major financial centres such as London, New York or Frankfurt. But in these cities, the beat system, which has evolved since the early days of business newspapers, has many of the characteristics of a club. 'Beats have their own protocols, timetables, events and inhibitions: active reporters will often expand and question these, less active ones will tend to accept the definitions of the area given by the most prominent players in it,' according to the media commentator and author and director of journalism at the Reuters Institute John Lloyd in January 2011. 'All beats tend to conservatism – both in seeking to extend the life of a beat which is no longer worth the coverage, and more seriously in not recognising new areas which should get specialist attention.'

The media's system of beats has made life easier for the club of PR firms hired to protect the reputations of companies in different sectors. And beat reporters found it convenient and useful to turn to PR firms which they knew had specialist knowledge of their sectors. For most of the history of the PR industry, it has not been an adversarial relationship. Rather, practitioners on both sides evolved into a stance of mutual dependency, each side observing the club rules.

When the rules of the club break down – such as when a company deliberately misleads its beat reporters, as Enron and WorldCom did for several years, and as Fannie Mae and Freddie Mac did at the height of the sub-prime crisis – there is often a period of retribution, or just sulking, by the media over allegedly 'dark' PR tactics.

The reality of the club is different, and more nuanced. The real rules rely on a properly executed flow of information and relationships of trust. It is not about power and access, even though some old-school PR agents might think it is. A managing partner of one international firm explains the distinction succinctly, saying:

> PR agencies are information brokers between their clients and the media. Good ones oil the wheels of understanding, bad ones obstruct it. It is no different with journalists: good ones help you understand the world, bad ones get in the way. It is utterly fallacious to believe that journalists have a common purpose and identity – holding power to account – while PRs are somehow forces for the dark side, trying to obscure understanding.
>
> At risk of exaggerating, there are some journalists and PRs who worship at the altar of power, and there are some who worship at the altar of truth. This is the real divide – not between journalists and PRs, but between those interested in truth and those in thrall to power.

For most of the 22 years from the City's 'Big Bang' to the Lehman collapse of 2008, the rules of the club tended to work pretty effectively. It was fairly easy to identify those agencies or PR executives for whom power came before truth, just as it was fairly straightforward to name the media outlets concerned with the veracity of a story rather than its power to shake markets. Members of all the respective clubs – the media, the bankers, the lawyers, the PR firms – broadly co-existed and fed off each other.

But the rules – already strained by scandals such as Enron – started to break down with the series of corporate crises that began in 2008 with the collapse of Lehman and the near-death experiences at a series of other institutions from Royal Bank of Scotland to Northern Rock. The business ecosystem was shaken further by corporate crises over subsequent years, from BP to

Toyota, and from News Corp to Nokia. Amid the reputational wreckage of such troubled companies, different members of the business clubs – especially in the PR and media world – were left looking at each other, asking whether the rules of the club still applied. Traditional ways of working together had fractured. Different rules were evolving. It was a new era in corporate communications: it was the dawn of the crisis cycle.

PART TWO

The Reckoning

CHAPTER 8

Crisis, What Crisis?

The chief executive was nervous. He had seen the recording of Tony Hayward's 2010 testimony to the US Congress. In that fateful encounter, his BP counterpart was verbally mauled on live TV. Hayward was accused of ducking questions, stalling and 'copping out' by the powerful House Committee on Energy and Commerce.

Facing scrutiny in a different sector, this chief executive was determined to avoid the same fate. He did not want to be 'spliced and diced' – as one Congressman had threatened Hayward. He certainly did not want to be told, in front of a worldwide audience, that: 'You're kicking the can down the road like you have nothing to do with this company', as reported in the *Daily Telegraph* on 17 July 2010.

So a large meeting room was booked at a downtown hotel in Washington DC. Furniture was re-arranged. TV cameras and spotlights were rigged up. And the layout of Committee Room 2123 in the Rayburn Building, a short walk from the Capitol, was recreated for a dress rehearsal. Partners of the corporation's law firm acted out the roles of committee members. PR advisers pretended to be journalists, ready to thrust a microphone or camera into the chief executive's face as he finished his testimony. The play-acting was serious; the questions were firm but fair. The corporation's reputation was on the line, and its executives could not afford any mishap when they faced the real committee a few days later.

At companies around the world, crisis preparation and avoidance strategies have gained new urgency following the humiliations suffered in recent years by a line-up of large corporations. Boardroom anxiety has been heightened by the public lambasting of corporate conduct by political committees on both sides of the Atlantic, of which Tony Hayward's congressional grilling was the most difficult.

On 15 February 2011, the *FT* quoted Andrew Caesar-Gordon, managing director of Electric Airwaves, an agency specialising in media training for political hearings, in a piece entitled 'Lessons in political correctness': 'CEOs in particular are not used to being badgered in the way that politicians often [are]. In their business lives – with the possible exception of interaction with the media or a court – meetings usually see the CEO with the upper hand.'

The growing prevalence of corporate crises played out in the full spotlight of media attention has fuelled demand for dress rehearsals, in turn spawning a cottage industry of small agencies focused wholly on executive coaching and training. The *Financial Times*, in the same article, reporting the growth in this business, cites training experts claiming that mock questioning tends to reveal potential flaws. 'One consultant relates the story of an executive who became so angry at one of his fake interviewers that his face flushed red – which showed up all the more in front of TV cameras. The practice session demonstrated to him the importance of controlling his temper for the real event.'

But no training manual or rehearsal can prevent the crises themselves, or reduce the outrage felt by politicians and the media at true corporate failure. This sense of crisis, which has dramatically changed the nature of financial public relations, has at its root a breakdown in trust. And that breakdown dates back to the global financial crisis of 2007–08, which marked the beginning of the end in traditional PR–media interaction. It was induced by the shock in the media and investor community at the scale of the credit crisis, which most commentators had failed to see coming and many of whom blamed partly on PR for blinding them to the problems infecting the financial system.

The truth is that PR played little or no part in hiding the scale of the crisis. If the agency world and in-house communications specialists were guilty of anything, it was a failure to be able to explain adequately what was going on or to have a crisis plan to protect their clients. And they failed to restore trust in their activities once the dam burst.

Explaining the erosion of trust, David M. Smick, the author and financial markets consultant, told the Aspen Institute's 'Ideas Festival' on 30 June 2009 at the height of the crisis:

> Perhaps the greatest mystery of this Great Credit Crisis is how some mortgage defaults in a relatively small sub-prime market (initially of only $200–300 billion) could topple a world financial system worth several hundred trillion dollars. How could some collapsing mortgages bring about the worst financial crisis since the 1930s?
>
> The answer is that the credit crisis reflected something larger and more fundamental than a mere problem of mortgage defaults. The crisis grew to such magnitude in large part because global markets declared a buyers' strike against our less than transparent financial archi-tecture – the sophisticated paper assets including secu-ritization that financial institutions use to measure risk and deploy capital. The housing crisis was a mere trig-ger for a collapse in trust of paper, followed by a delever-aging of the entire bloated-with-credit financial system.

The collapse in trust, initially in the financial system, began to spread to broader corporate conduct with a sharp decline in investor confidence. Distrust of paper and the conduct of banks infected media attitudes to other companies. In a climate of panic at falling stock markets, fuelled by media reporting that the global economy was at the abyss, each new corporate crisis gained a momentum unseen prior to 2008.

BP was, arguably, one of the companies whose situation con-tributed to general corporate mistrust following the Deepwater Horizon accident in 2010. The company suffered a reputation

meltdown because of a two-fold lack of preparation: its PR relationship building in the USA prior to the disaster was weak, and
there was a glaring gap between where the company thought it
was in terms of US public opinion and the reality.

'What changed was that Barack Obama went for Tony
Hayward personally and suggested that BP should pay for the
costs of the entire drilling moratorium in the Gulf,' according
to one of the oil company's PR advisers. 'The stakes were high
and investors panicked. It was a battle for survival because 40
per cent of the BP stock was in the US, and half of that was in US
pension funds – many of which thought there was no way back.'

The result was a six-stage crisis communications effort to
help save the company, which one BP insider described as a full-
blown political campaign. The six parts of the plan involved a
systematic management scheme for the media, domestic and
international; an investor relations drive to reassure shareholders that BP would survive; a public affairs scheme to mend
bridges in Washington DC; a sophisticated digital 'war room'
to engage with bloggers, social media and the Twitter community; a specific game-plan for dealing with the Obama administration; and a crisis scenario 'roadmap' to anticipate future
reputation risks until the well was capped and beyond that as
the company sought to repair its profile around the world. But
that plan emerged only after BP had ignored its own crisis handbook, which called for a steering group to be formed immediately to oversee all aspects of any disaster response.

The BP experience exposed a lack of readiness for the crisis that engulfed the company and an initial reaction in which
communications strategies made things worse rather than better. The same was true of Toyota, McKinsey, Maclaren, Netflix,
News Corp, Olympus, Nokia and others which suffered separate
crises in the 2008–12 four-year business cycle.

Jeffrey Liker and Timothy Ogden, an academic and a communications consultant following the Toyota story, concluded
that Toyota's problems of 2009–10 – when the company recalled

more than 6.5 million cars to fix incorrectly fitted floor mats and sticky accelerator pedals – were more to do with poor communications and a Japanese management culture unused to global media scrutiny of supposed vehicle safety problems. In their book, *Toyota under Fire*, Liker and Ogden revealed that although Toyota was a leader in manufacturing standards it did not have a crisis communication function. Toyota couched its recall notices and other communications in dispassionate, technical language in keeping with its culture of fact-based decision-making. But this made it sound out of touch.[11]

Nearly 18 months after the Toyota recall, the company was largely vindicated and investigators found no problems with its electronics. But it has had to battle hard to rehabilitate its image, particularly with a US media audience frustrated at its slow responsiveness.

Toyota's experience exposed another worrying front in the new era of crisis communications: it is impossible to manage media expectations in a 24-hour digital news cycle when the outcome of investigations might take months or years to complete. Stephen Carver, a lecturer in project management at the Cranfield School of Management in the UK, in the *FT* of 14 June 2011, explains the dilemma as a timing issue for companies that can't explain their case in time to meet the demands of a hungry media. 'The stakes are much higher nowadays if you make a corporate blunder. Companies used to have more time to think before they had to react, but now they must respond immediately. Toyota's problem wasn't the technical one – product recalls are common in the car industry – but the fact that the company was too slow to respond.'

The same sort of slow response problem hit McKinsey when it emerged that Anil Kumar, one of its partners, was supplying inside information in return for kickbacks to Raj Rajaratnam, the hedge fund trader who was subsequently jailed for 11 years.

---

[11] Jeffrey Liker and Timothy Ogden, *Toyota under Fire: Lessons for Turning Crisis into Opportunity*, New York, McGraw-Hill, 2011.

McKinsey was forced on the defensive at the same time by claims by the Securities and Exchange Commission that Rajat Gupta, head of the firm from 1994–2003, was also passing on inside information to the same hedge fund operator. McKinsey was put on the communications defensive because its core operating mantra – trust and discretion – was being questioned.

Like McKinsey, another company in a completely different sector – Maclaren – was unprepared for the media tsunami that swept over the company after it announced in November 2009 that it was issuing repair kits for a million pushchairs sold in the USA over the prior ten years after a dozen children lost part of their fingers in the mechanism. The lesson of these crises, compounded in 2011 by the scandals at News Corp and Olympus among others, was that companies need to have far more robust crisis communications systems in place. They and their advisers also need to understand customer sentiment and digital reactions in a more sophisticated way. RIM, the Canadian smartphone manufacturer, faced similar calls to improve its responsiveness following a major network outage in 2011. 'For RIM, the network outage looks to be the result of a classic mix of technological complacency, poor disaster planning and a failure to grasp the basic principles of crisis management, beginning with the need for quick and clear communication by senior executives,' said Richard Waters, US west coast managing editor of the *FT*, in the issue for 15 October 2011.

In all of these cases, the core communication problems were related to a basic lack of trust in what companies were saying. The lack of confidence in business conduct meant that traditional crisis plans were largely ineffective for a fast-moving digital news cycle, in which reporters and other external audiences were often ready to make ill-judged assumptions based on partial facts or whistle-blower briefings. The breakdown of trust was compounded by companies failing to recognise the size of the threat or the risk it posed to their long-term reputations. Too often they saw themselves as victims of a problem caused by others – in some cases companies seemed to blame their own suppliers, contractors and even customers – rather than assuming responsibility at the outset and sorting out liability later on.

All of this was made worse by a culture in many companies, and among some of their advisers, of not reporting bad news upwards. Part of the licence to operate for an outside consultant is the ability to tell your client ugly news, and to tell them they are behaving badly. But firms are so anxious to preserve their retained relationships that some are reluctant to give hard advice.

In turn, a number of crises have been affected by a blame game on the part of clients and advisers. Valuable time is wasted trying to pin the problems on individuals or business operations that were not acting within a company's supposed rules. Costa Cruises, the shipping company that operated the capsized *Costa Concordia* liner, was among the latest companies to fall into the blame game in 2012 when it accused its ship's captain, Francesco Schettino, of responsibility for the disaster off the Italian island of Giglio in January 2012. In passenger cruises, so-called 'thrill diversions' of the type that holed the *Concordia*, are not uncommon – so the cruise company could be exposed by trying to make its captain take all of the blame.

Such controversies have created a sense of bewilderment for many corporate boards, which are alarmed at how quickly their carefully built reputations can be shredded. They have also caused consternation among some traditional PR companies, which have found that their old rules for media engagement do not necessarily help in a full-blown digital cycle.

Ironically, however, the crises have been massively profitable for the agencies handling the problems. Crisis fees have filled a valuable hole left by the decline in mergers and acquisitions, with troubled clients willing to pay almost any price to save their reputations. Clients pay hefty fees because they trust their advisers to fix the problem, to mend their broken profiles.

But in a period when trust is in short supply – between clients and their customers, between the media and PR advisers

– the crises have forced a broader rethink of the PR approach to problem-solving. It has opened the market to agencies that do nothing but crisis management, and created a platform for new firms to launch with a more sophisticated approach to reputation risk management.

The arrival of the risk managers in the PR industry has heralded a new approach to communications.

Firms born in a post-Lehman fully digital world have a different approach to their legacy competitors. The new firms assume that investor confidence is shaky and that the media has lost trust in many areas of corporate conduct, so companies need to get better at identifying and managing areas of reputation risk before they arise. Reactive advice, after a crisis has broken, remains critical to a company's well-being. But avoidance advice, which prevents a problem becoming a communications disaster, is becoming even more valuable. Such advice – anticipatory and diagnostic – is an increasingly important tool for companies nervous about their reputations. These companies know that they can no longer approach any sort of communications threat with a sense of bereavement. The age of denial is finally over.

CHAPTER 9

The Five Stages of Grief

Financial communications specialists love their vernacular. Crises are routinely 'shit storms'; disputes between advisers are 'cluster-fucks'. Meeting rooms are 'fish bowls', reputations are 'fragile flowers' and doing your job is 'a licence to operate'. Then there are the acronyms: the RoI – return on investment; the PBTs – profit before taxes; M&A for mergers and acquisitions; and a long list including Ebit, CSR, Swots, PE multiples and, of course, PR itself.

But now the industry is coming to terms with 'DABDA' – a new and painful adjustment faced by all companies in crisis. DABDA has long been familiar to bereavement counsellors. But its application to corporate reputation is new and pertinent. Tony Hayward has certainly been through it. James Murdoch is still wrestling with it. Mike Lazaridis and Jim Balsillie resigned as joint chief executives of Research in Motion because they didn't get through it.

DABDA is the acronym applied to the work of Swiss-born psychiatrist Elisabeth Kübler-Ross in her acclaimed work, *On Death and Dying*.[12] In it, she defined the five stages of grief as denial, anger, bargaining, depression and acceptance – hence DABDA. Originally conceived to help individuals come to terms with the loss of a loved one, it has also become a useful metaphor for how companies or individual executives deal with crises.

There have been numerous high-profile sufferers of corporate grief in recent years, affecting the careers of individual executives or the companies they lead. The denial, anger, bargaining, depression and final acceptance affects corporations in a wide range of industries over failed deals, flawed strategies

---

[12] E. Kübler-Ross, *On Death and Dying*, London, Tavistock, 1970.

or the exposure of personal mistakes that can be fatal for high profile careers.

In recent years, those going through the corporate equivalent of DABDA have included Fred Goodwin, the former chief executive of Royal Bank of Scotland, who was stripped of his knighthood in 2012 for his role in the banking crisis. There was the collective bereavement among executives at Olympus of Japan, the scandal-hit camera and medical equipment company. Lloyd C. Blankfein, the Goldman Sachs chief executive, acknowledged his own DABDA journey when he told a New York conference in 2009 that the bank had reached the acceptance stage in its grieving process. 'We participated in things that were clearly wrong and have reason to regret,' he said.

In some cases, corporate grief is followed by personal grief in a depressing cycle. Hence, Lord Browne, the former chief executive of BP, argued in 2007 that his focus on repairing the image of the oil company in the wake of the Texas City refinery and Alaska pipeline disasters distracted him from dealing with a personal relationship that would overshadow the end of his BP career.

Lord Browne, regarded as an icon of British industry, was suffering the first stage of grief for his career: this can't be happening to me. He was angry at newspaper intrusion into his private life and failed in the bargaining phase: a legal attempt to prevent publication. Depression, the fourth stage, probably followed after one of Britain's leading judges, a specialist in privacy hearings, criticised the BP chief for misleading the High Court with his initial witness statement. By the time the game was up, and Lord Browne decided he had no option but to resign, he was beyond depression. He was remarkably calm. Former colleagues recall that there were tears in the BP boardroom, but not from Browne. He agreed the text of a brief press release, signed the letters to staff, and watched with detachment as the business channels led their bulletins with his departure. He had accepted his fate.

'I felt hurt, absolutely, but you know it is what it is,' he said later, in the *FT* of 17 February 2012. It 'created an extraordinary chain of events which I didn't handle well, the press didn't handle well; then you say to yourself, in the words of my mother, who had real reason to say it [she was deported to Auschwitz as a child and Lord Browne's grandparents were killed], "Don't trust anybody".'

Such corporate and personal grief – particularly at the actions perpetrated by the media – is nothing new. Back in the Great Crash of 1929, all five stages of grief were on display almost on a daily basis as stock markets collapsed. 'Clerks in downtown hotels were said to be asking guests whether they wished the room for sleeping or jumping. Two men jumped hand-in-hand from a high window in the Ritz. They had a joint account,' wrote J.K. Galbraith.[13] At the time, the financial editor of the *New York Times* commented: 'Probably none of the present generation will be able to speak again of a "healthy reaction". There are many signs that the phrase is entirely out of date.'

The various stages of corporate grief, ranging from the despair in Japan at the 2011 earthquake that killed thousands and disrupted production for entire industries, to the anger at the exposure of criminal wrongdoing at News International newspapers in the UK, or the depression induced by corporate scandals such as the 2001 implosion of Enron, have forced advisers to large companies to behave increasingly like bereavement counsellors. That is why a growing number of communications advisers, particularly at the boardroom level, these days liken themselves to therapists.

Many of those advisers would identify with the work of Colin Murray Parkes, the revered UK psychiatrist and bereavement expert. In his seminal work, *Bereavement: Studies of Grief in Adult Life*, Parkes could have been referring to the PR advice offered to senior executives at disaster-hit companies when he wrote:

---

[13] J.K. Galbraith, *The Great Crash, 1929*, London, Hamish Hamilton, 1955.

'It is a principle of crisis intervention that help given at a time when pathological patterns of thought and behaviour are developing is likely to be more acceptable and more effective than help given a long time after these pathological patterns have become established.'[14]

Just like the bereaved individuals treated by Parkes and other psychiatrists, the grief-stricken in the business world need protection, reassurance, time to recoup, and help in developing blueprints for the future. 'Those who are in a position to meet these needs must expect to find the recipient of their help defensive, sensitive, vulnerable, and unreasonable,' according to Parkes, in another refrain familiar to senior corporate advisers.

Such willingness to accept help at times of crisis – to acknowledge the need for PR therapy – assumes that the bereaved are beyond the denial or anger stages of DABDA. The mood of defensiveness, bordering on despair, and anger at perceived unfair treatment are common behaviour patterns during most corporate crises. And often that despair and anger is turned on the advisers, who find themselves being blamed for making things worse rather than better.

Farzad Rastegar, the chief executive of Maclaren, the baby equipment manufacturer, felt that PR advice exacerbated the furore over the company's US recall of faulty pushchairs in which children's fingers were being pinched, bruised, cut or even partially amputated. 'The negative reaction was like an explosion from one market to the next,' recalled Mr Rastegar in the *Harvard Business Review* of January 2011. 'We did hire a big PR firm in the middle of the crisis, but that, too, turned out to be a mistake. The firm's advice – which ranged from making an apology to limiting my personal appearances because of my foreign accent (I'm of Persian origin) – was out of line with my desire to defend the fundamental safety of our products and to communicate directly and openly with our customers.'

---

[14] C.M. Parkes, *Bereavement: Studies of Grief in Adult Life*, London, Tavistock, 1972.

It took almost a year for the Maclaren boss to get from denial and anger through to acceptance. By the time he did, he was ready to thank various stakeholders including parents, retailers and employees for continuing to support the brand in spite of the tidal wave of damaging media coverage. And Mr Rastegar even took some solace from the saga. It was a reminder, he said, to emphasise a safety-first culture, to become more cohesive as a management team and 'we have realized that Maclaren must play a bigger leadership role in the industry, mobilizing other brands, manufacturers, retailers, and regulators around the world to work toward mandatory minimum global standards with common definitions, harmonized procedures, and uniform protocols.'

Like an increasing number of senior executives, Mr Rastegar now accepts that the bereavement process relating to Maclaren's reputation would have been easier if the company had been better prepared for the scale of the crisis. But it often takes a crisis for a company to review the quality of its PR readiness – and then only once the company has reached the 'acceptance phase' as its grief subsides. Only then, it seems, are they ready to acknowledge the problems affecting their companies, and ready to embark on whatever reorganisation – and in many cases resignations – that might be necessary to deal with a particular problem. Until that point, PR advisers find themselves on the receiving end of the 'bargaining phase' of the grieving process: 'we will pay you handsomely to make this problem go away'.

As with real bereavement, the denial phase can last for years, and the anger can be furious to behold. The Enron saga, in particular, was characterised by significant internal denial and anger at the allegations sweeping over the company before its spectacular crash. The sheer disbelief of senior managers prevented the company from accepting the scale of its problems, stopping the communications advisers both inside and outside the company from doing their jobs. 'This is a company

entering into a crisis,' Mark Palmer, Enron's head of public relations (and now a partner at Brunswick), told an internal executive meeting as the allegations mounted. Kurt Eichenwald, the
New York Times correspondent who charted Enron's downfall,
described the denial and anger in scrupulous detail:

> For any kind of crisis management, Palmer said, there
> were three *As* – acknowledge, apologize, and act. The
> company had to acknowledge there was a problem,
> apologize for whatever it had done to cause it, and then
> present a plan of action to fix it.
>
> At that, the room exploded. 'We're not apologizing
> for anything!' John Lavorato, a top trader roared.
>
> 'Absolutely not!' chimed in another senior executive,
> Dave Delainey. 'There's nothing wrong with Enron. We
> don't owe anyone an apology for anything!'
>
> Palmer shot them a look. 'Well,' he said, 'will you
> acknowledge that we've got a crisis?'
>
> Delainey folded his arms. 'What do we have to
> acknowledge?'
>
> Palmer threw up his hands. 'Dave! The stock is drop-
> ping like a rock. No one trusts what we say, with things
> now at the point that people who don't like us are leak-
> ing information they think will be damaging to us. The
> *Wall Street Journal* wants to write a story about us. *And
> we're not cooperating with them!*[15]

This sort of exchange should resonate with public relations
executives dealing with companies in turmoil. It is a fair bet that
similar conversations have been played out in recent years at a
range of other companies, although few have collapsed in spectacular fashion like Enron. That turmoil has claimed even more
corporate victims in recent years. They have included corporate

---

[15] Kurt Eichenwald, *Conspiracy of Fools*, New York, Broadway Books, 2005.

minnows and some of the largest fish in the business ocean – among them UBS, Siemens and Netflix.

UBS, the Swiss banking group, suffered a severe bereavement over an alleged $2.3 billion rogue trading scandal that ultimately led to the departure of its powerful chief executive Oswald Grübel in September 2011. In his resignation memo to staff, Grübel acknowledges the grief felt inside the bank, writing: 'That it was possible for one of our traders in London to inflict a multi-billion loss on our bank shocked me, as it did everyone else, deeply. This incident has worldwide repercussions, including political ones. I did not take the step of resigning lightly. I am convinced that it is in the interests of UBS to approach the future with a new leader at the top.'

His successor, Sergio Ermotti, subsequently tried to help UBS staff through the grieving process with a follow-up memo, also reported in *The Guardian* of 24 September 2011, urging them to be stoical: 'Speculation regarding what occurred is likely to continue for some time yet. Our clients, colleagues and friends will ask legitimate questions to which we won't always have the answers at the time. Please do not allow yourselves to get involved in speculation. We will ensure that you receive material to support you in such conversations.'

At times of crisis, such memos – formulated jointly by legal and PR advisers – are an important part of the strategy to manage the grief felt by employees. At companies where the primary product is the quality of its people, such as in banking and management consultancy, employee confidence is even more important and requires deft communications skills.

Any failure to communicate internally, any failure to manage public relations inside a company, poses significant risks. And even the most revered companies are not immune to a crisis of confidence. McKinsey is among a cluster of highly regarded organisations that have been trying to rebuild such confidence. The management consultancy has been grieving for its reputation ever since a scandal in 2010, in which its former boss was accused of passing inside information to a criminal hedge fund trader. Rajat Gupta, who led the company between 1994 and 2003, denied any wrongdoing. 'But the very fact that a former leader's conduct has been questioned has shaken McKinsey's 1300 partners. "Anger, disbelief, shock, sadness and outrage," is how one describes the mood,' reported the *FT* on 10 March 2011.

Usually, such expressions of grief are relished by the media, seizing on a corporate fall from grace, speculating about compensation packages, the boardroom battles and the reputation fallout. In the current crisis cycle, which has challenged the entire corporate PR world to improve the quality of its service, the media has been virulent in its condemnation of bad behaviour. Executives complain loudly and frequently to their advisers about erroneous and sometimes vicious reporting.

But the irony of the crisis years, from 2008–12, has been that the media has itself suffered a collective bereavement for its reputation and its entire future. Even before the phone-hacking scandal exploded at News International, the media industry was grief-stricken by a wave of newspaper closures or redundancies as a combination of tumbling circulation, volatile advertising, rising costs and digital competition exposed fault lines across the sector. In a 2008 speech in London, Bill Keller of the *New York Times* captured the sense of grief, saying: 'At places where editors and publishers gather, the mood these days is funereal. Editors ask one another, "How are you?" in that sober tone one employs with friends who have just emerged from rehab or a messy divorce.'

The business threat to print media and difficult trading conditions for broadcast news have coincided with a general erosion of trust in journalism. That erosion has been underway for years. At the turn of the century, less than 30 per cent of Americans said they could believe all or most media reporting, according to the Pew Research Center's annual *State of the News Media* for 2011. But that figure was below 20 per cent by the end of the decade. The same trend, only worse, has been seen in the

UK. In 2009, Britain's Media Standards Trust reported that only 7 per cent of people believed that national newspapers behaved responsibly, while 75 per cent of those polled claimed that newspapers regularly publish inaccurate stories.

Levels of mistrust are likely to decline even further following the News International scandal, in which a culture of illegal phone-hacking and corrupt payments to public officials has been exposed and subjected to a public inquiry. 'Reporters, writers, editors and printers are wandering round like victims of a bomb blast, enveloped in a cloud of digital dust. The profession of journalism staggers about, choking for air. Nobody knows quite what is happening,' according to Simon Jenkins, former editor of *The Times*, writing in *The Guardian* on 6 July 2011. 'Continued revelation of the reporting practices of the News of the World suggest the bomb was a suicide. Editors on a paper whose stock in trade is human anguish appeared to lose all respect for the law, let alone self-control.'

The crisis and grief in journalism, under way for several years but now exacerbated by scandal, has further raised fundamental questions about media relevance. In turn, that is posing a major threat to PR companies. If the media is less trusted, less influential and increasingly irrelevant to a world of digital discourse, then what is the relevance of a PR industry built on media engagement?

For the time being, clients both individual and corporate seem to believe that more advice, not less, is needed in an era where the news media takes more risks and places less store by accuracy. Falling trust and dwindling audiences for the media, however, pose a threat that extends beyond news organisations themselves. The sense of bereavement may soon spread to public relations if clients begin to question the quality, cost and relevance of the advice they receive. If the PR industry fails to manage client expectations correctly during this uncertain period, it could soon find itself going through DABDA. This may be an industry facing five stages of grief.

CHAPTER 10

Media in Peril

Asense of grief and grievance is sweeping through journalism. Leading media outlets in some of the world's largest capital markets, a prime target for the PR industry, are suffering collective self-doubt over the worsening economics of newspapers, broadcast news and magazine publishing. That unease has been compounded by the reputational damage inflicted on the news industry by rogue reporters, primarily at Britain's scandal-hit News International. The wrongdoing has fuelled a sense of grievance among reporters who have seen their trade accused of criminal wrongdoing and threatened with tougher regulation.

But there is no cheering in the financial PR industry, which has often enjoyed a combative relationship with news outlets. For PR agencies are locked into a supply-side relationship with the news media, for which their clients pay handsome fees for the ability to negotiate with potentially troublesome reporters. If those reporters, or the outlets they work for, are losing influence and readership, then there could be a damaging knock-on effect for the many PR executives whose relevance is inextricably tied to delivering coverage.

The upheaval in the media industry has, therefore, begun to alarm the communications advisers and their clients, who face an uncertain outcome from both the structural change in news economics and the cyclical swing towards editorial risk-taking. The net result is that businesses hoping to manage their reputations effectively have fewer opportunities to do so. It is simple mathematics. Today, there are fewer media outlets with fewer business pages. Increasingly desperate journalists are fighting over editorial space. So they take risks with stories of dubious quality, hoping to secure a prime piece of print or broadcast real estate. And the amount of space available has been further reduced by columnist inflation, with more and more pages devoted to commentary. Further up the supply chain, companies are no longer guaranteed coverage of their regular financial results or other announcements. PR agencies, at least in developed Western markets, can no longer offer clients any assurance about likely media interest. And the scepticism among reporters about their own industry's future is starting to adversely affect the coverage of other sectors in turmoil.

This upheaval is posing a major problem for the PR industry. For generations, the main interface between financial PR agencies and the media was through newspapers. But the future of newspapers is under threat in a digital world of fragmenting advertising revenues, freely available online content and a migration of readers to other sources of news. This disturbing trend was evident before the current wave of corporate crisis, which began with the collapse of Lehman Brothers and which has accelerated in subsequent years. Writing in 2008, the year of Lehman's demise, US columnist Eric Alterman captured the seismic changes in the newspaper industry – which has affected every reader, every business and every intermediary engaged with the media. In the *New Yorker* of 31 March 2008, he claimed:

> To own the dominant, or only, newspaper in a mid-sized American city was, for many decades, a kind of license to print money. In the Internet age, however, no one has figured out how to rescue the newspaper in the United States or abroad. Newspapers have created websites that benefit from the growth of online advertising, but the sums are not nearly enough to replace the loss in revenue from circulation and print ads.
>
> Most managers in the industry have reacted to the collapse of their business model with a spiral of budget cuts, bureau closings, buyouts, lay-offs, and reductions

in page size and column inches. Since 1990, a quarter of all American newspaper jobs have disappeared.

That trend has continued in recent years, with print circulation continuing to decline for most titles in most mature markets. Advertising has remained volatile, and it has been hard for all but the most specialist titles to persuade subscribers to pay for online editions. *State of the News Media 2011: An Annual Report on American Journalism,* published by the Pew Research Center, warned that the economic problems facing newspapers were more severe than those of other media. It estimated that up to 1,500 newsroom jobs have disappeared in the past decade. Researchers Tom Rosenstiel and Amy Mitchell of the Project for Excellence in Journalism concluded in the same report:

> Beneath all this, however, a more fundamental challenge to journalism became clearer in the last year. The biggest issue ahead may not be lack of audience or even lack of new revenue experiments. It may be that in the digital realm the news industry is no longer in control of its own future.
>
> News organizations – old and new – still produce most of the content audiences consume. But each technological advance has added a new layer of complexity – and a new set of players – in connecting that content to consumers and advertising.

This new ecosystem is affecting public relations, a sector built around managing the news. For most of its history, agencies in the mature markets of Western Europe and North America have relied on a linear engagement strategy with print media. The ability to protect and promote corporate reputations depended on direct influence, or at least dialogue, with influential newspaper titles. For generations, business journalists and PR agencies tended to observe certain codes of behaviour. Everyone knew the distinction between 'off-the-record' and background briefing. Everyone knew when newspapers went to bed, and when journalists were available. The evolution of a business story from press release to front-page news was fairly simple and easy to predict. The deadlines and rules of engagement were accepted by all sides.

All that changed in the digital era. Newspapers have cut pagination, or closed down altogether, or moved to a web-first strategy. It has altered fundamentally the old rules of PR combat. That transition is especially marked in the USA, but is also replicated in the UK and neighbouring countries. In one generation, UK newspaper circulation has tumbled. Among tabloids, sales of the *Daily Mirror* have declined from 4.2 million a day to about 1 million. Figures cited by Peter Preston, former editor of *The Guardian* and now media columnist for *The Observer*, suggest that the broadsheet *Daily Telegraph* has lost more than half its daily sales, compared with the 1970s, and most other titles have suffered double-digit declines.

Similar weakness has affected publications in Italy, France, Spain and Germany – changing the rules of engagement for PR firms there too. In Germany, the threat caused by digital fragmentation persuaded newspaper publishers to seek legal protection for their future. In the so-called Hamburg Declaration of June 2009, major publishing houses called for an expansion of copyright law to protect publishers against search engines' increased dominance of the internet.

The PR industry, similarly, finds itself torn between traditional media relationships with publishers in markets such as Germany and the opportunities to reach new audiences on digital platforms. But even if agencies prefer the media 'devil they know', they cannot ignore the changes to media economics in countries such as the UK, Germany and France.

In France, similar concerns have surfaced about online media migration following sharp falls in print advertising, leading to editorial job cuts and bureau closures. The French media upheaval has been exacerbated by the growth in free newspapers, with *20Minutes* and *Metro* now boasting circulation ahead of *Le Monde* and *Le Figaro*. 'Publishers are responding to the crisis by cutting costs. Pages are fewer and editorial offices are emptying as part of a major trend,' according to one French publisher.

For most newspapers, this rate of decline has not yet been offset completely by explosive growth in digital revenues, even for specialist titles such as the *Wall Street Journal* and *Financial Times*, whose subscribers are more willing to pay for online content. Doubters of the digital model suspect that even these titles have been trading 'analogue dollars for digital pennies'. Until relatively recently, for example, it was possible to buy every piece of advertising space on FT.com for a week for less than the cost of one page in the newspaper on one day. That problematic equation is hitting all print titles.

The deteriorating economics of news journalism is forcing publishers to cut back on day-to-day corporate coverage. Fewer companies see their earnings covered on a quarterly basis. Page leads are determined not by statutory figures, but by whatever new angle can be found in a press release or earnings statement. This, in turn, is forcing PR agencies to reconsider their strategies. The old command and control rules, insofar as they ever existed, have largely disappeared in a world of limited space for news reporting and an increasing shift in the media's centre of gravity to opinion-based commentary. In the UK alone, the number of national newspaper columnists has increased by 50 per cent to more than 300 in the past decade. Editorial Intelligence, the media analysis firm, claims these columnists are generating more than 50,000 words of comment each day.

The rise of the commentators at the expense of space for news coverage poses both an opportunity and a threat to the PR industry. A favourable opinion column is far more valuable to an agency and its client than a straightforward news report. But columnists on the *FT*'s Lex desk, Breakingviews or the *Wall Street Journal*'s Heard-on-the-Street section are notoriously hard to manage. The ability to place an opinion column on the editorial pages of leading outlets has become harder still, with hundreds of would be pundits chasing a handful of slots every week.

The media's turmoil is a major worry for the intermediaries trying to shape opinions in the new ecosystem of digital news and commentary. Marcus Brauchli, executive editor of the *Washington Post*, argues that journalists, business leaders, advisers and media owners are still trying to figure out how to interact in the new digital ecosystem. In the 3rd Richard S. Salant Lecture on freedom of the press, given at Harvard University on 28 October 2010, Brauchli said:

> Now suddenly we all inhabit the same digital realm. How we differentiate ourselves is in our approaches to information journalism. Here, too, newcomers co-exist alongside traditional players. So for example right- and left-wing poison pen political bloggers co-exist alongside fanatic political news aggregators and specialized political news websites which, in turn, co-exist alongside traditional newsrooms that cover politics...
>
> Now this ecosystem is not necessarily a harmonious place. Indeed there is a lot not to love about new media, especially those who cloak their ideological agendas in journalistic garb or those who depend for their existence on others' work.

The PR industry and its corporate clients have been trying to map out how this new ecosystem affects their business, and whether it is a welcome development or a frightening one. For most, fear currently outweighs optimism about the changing media engagement. The structural changes to newspaper economics are something that agency executives, particularly the former journalists among them, can identify with. Business correspondents are trying to do their job in a far more difficult atmosphere, with less time to research stories or with fewer opportunities to meet companies or to check story accuracy. But that is no comfort to company executives, who sense that journalists are sometimes beyond briefing in their race to post stories online ahead of their equally overstretched competitors.

Critics of the PR industry claim that unscrupulous operators are exploiting editorial vulnerabilities caused by the economic maelstrom sweeping the media industry. Nick Davies, the *Guardian* journalist who has exposed much of the wrongdoing at News International, argues that a PR conveyor belt is taking advantage of the pressures on news organisations:

> For many decades, news editors and reporters used 'news values' and contacts to decide what stories to run. Now, to a decisive extent, that crucial process of news judgement has been taken out of their hands. Indeed, it has been taken right outside of their organisations, so that routinely they find themselves processing stories which have been chosen for them by people whose job is to shape news coverage in the service of powerful interests, whether commercial, political or other.[16]

He goes on to argue: 'This is not just about PR inserting the material which it chooses: it also involves suppressing the stories which might cause embarrassment to its clients.' As evidence, he cites an estimated 30 per cent compound annual increase in the size of the PR industry, and an investigation by *Columbia Journalism Review* which found that in one edition of the *Wall Street Journal* more than half of the news stories 'were based solely on press releases'.

Such claims imply that news organisations are increasingly passive recipients of PR manipulation, which some agencies would relish if it were true. In reality, the dog-fights between business journalists willing to take risks and PR agencies

---

[16] Nick Davies, *Flat Earth News*, London, Vintage, 2009.

seeking to protect reputations have never been more aggressive. 'Mature companies and PRs are not looking to pull the wool over people's eyes – they are happy with fact-based responsible journalism,' says a partner of one London firm. 'The scariest journalist is the person who is trying to make a name for themself; who is cavalier with the facts and trying to make a story fit a preconceived agenda. That sin which afflicts a lot of UK journalism also affects business journalism.'

Some media observers believe this 'sin' is not confined to maverick journalists at the riskier end of newsgathering. They believe it is a secular trend, which is linked to both the strained economics of today's media and an imperative to deliver more spectacular scoops. The exposure at News International of phone-hacking, illegal payments to public officials and a hyper-aggressive news culture has also instilled fear into business leaders who worry that their conduct may be the next target of a news-pack searching hungrily for the next big story.

Simon Jenkins, former editor of *The Times*, a News International title, believes that the scandal is a wake-up call for journalism that represents a pivotal moment for the industry. 'For all newspapers, the News of the World phone-hacking scandal has become a moment of truth. It has shown how far commercial pressure from the web and from within big corporations has distorted ethics,' he argued in *The Guardian* on 6 July 2011. 'Journalism has always tested the bounds of investigatory intrusion, but it cannot break or interfere with legal process … The case for a continuing profession of journalism is that there is public value in the marshalling and editing of information by disciplined media institutions such as newspapers and broadcasters.'

Businesses around the world are increasingly fearful of the pressures on news media, and how they will affect coverage of their organisations – particularly at times of crisis or populist campaigns against executive remuneration, consumer pricing or product reliability. Most executives also recognise that their

PR agencies are finding it harder, indeed riskier, to seek media influence or guarantee certain types of coverage. Any sense of manipulation or undue pressure has the opposite impact in a media community already suffering an inferiority complex.

This is creating a paradox. Although traditional news media outlets are losing readers and cutting corporate coverage, business leaders are as concerned as ever about what is written about them. They are anxious to avoid being lumped together with rival companies, some of whom might be facing crisis or weakening demand. They dislike the eroding experience and churn among reporters on corporate beats, many of whom have no time or background to grasp the complexity of different industries. And they are particularly un-nerved by the immediacy of online judgments, which even when news outlets acknowledge inaccuracy are hard to remove from the lingering reach of search engines.

Their PR advisers are trying to offer some reassurance during the media transition. Their assurances often involve more focused engagement tactics. From the past service focused on managing the media and seeking positive reports, they are now targeting fewer, more analytical, and often less news-oriented types of coverage. Media engagement plans have become studies in damage limitation or risk management. Troublesome reporters are identified and avoided. But there is an emerging view across PR that 'media management' has become a contradiction in terms. The old codes of conduct with traditional media are strained. And an even greater challenge lies ahead: how to deal with digital and social networks.

CHAPTER 11

Digital Divide

Twenty years ago, the international editions of the *Financial Times* were assembled in London and faxed as complete broadsheet pages to remote print sites in Frankfurt and New York. The fax machines, each the size of a church organ, were regularly clogged with Tipp-Ex as harassed sub-editors rushed to correct typos or change headlines.

How the pages arrived was a mystery to many of the journalists working on the paper. The inner-workings of the fax machines were equally mysterious to the *FT*'s management. One director, faxing a letter to Frankfurt, told his secretary: 'It's a confidential fax, so put it in an envelope.' Within a decade, the *FT* was dispatching multiple editions by satellite link to cities around the world. The daily timetable of global deadlines, feeding content to printers from Sydney to San Francisco, resembled a giant sudoku puzzle.

Today, the *FT* has abandoned remote printing in growth markets such as Brazil. Readers rely on digital editions, available to download, updated frequently by blogs, tweets, podcasts, videos and email alerts from multi-tasking reporters. The digitisation of such outlets is mirrored across the information industry, disaggregating traditional forms of content creation and news distribution.

'The world wide web fundamentally changed the media eco-system, challenging established journalistic practice in what is known as the mainstream media: radio, television, newspapers and magazines,' according to Lionel Barber, editor of the *Financial Times*, in the Fulbright Lecture, 'The Future of News and Newspapers in the Digital Revolution', given on 14 September 2011. 'As media experts such as Clay Shirky have noted: in an increasingly networked world, power has shifted from the publisher to the consumer. Passive consumers can turn into active publishers operating around the clock in the so-called blogosphere. The world is more anarchic, but also more democratic.'

The *FT* and other titles are now preparing for a potential world beyond print, given that the final copy of a printed newspaper could land on somebody's doorstep within 30 years. That demise is troubling for corporations and their PR advisers because it deprives the communications world of an easily understandable route to market.

The advisory community is adjusting – alongside the media – to a multi-platform environment of exploding access to information. The old 'push' system of PR distribution, in which clients and their advisers largely decided what information to release and when, has been replaced by a 'pull' mechanism in which global audiences including customers, the media, regulators, investors, politicians and others are firmly in control of how they consume all manner of news and content.

Information management is far harder in a world of proliferating technology and rapidly changing media consumption habits. 'Even small children know their way round the internet,' warns Sir Martin Sorrell, chief executive of WPP, the marketing services group that owns several large PR agencies. In their annual report for 2010, under the heading 'A fragmenting media', he says:

Decision-makers in media owners and agencies tend to be in their fifties and sixties; their children and grandchildren are shifting in ever greater numbers to multitasking on the web, personal video recorders (PVRs), video-on-demand, smart phones, iPods, video iPods, iPhones, iPads, Kindles, mobiles, podcasts and multiplayer internet games. Declining newspaper readership, particularly among younger people and the resultant collapse of established titles are alarming trends …

Many executives are in denial. They believe – or hope – that radical change will not happen on their watch.

The digital revolution is set to accelerate amid forecasts that global internet traffic is set to grow at 40–50 per cent a year. More of that traffic will be mobile, as content consumption shifts to the 2.5 billion smartphones expected to be in circulation by 2015. Already, this is transforming the potential information channels available to business. To put that in context, fibre optic cables are being tested that can carry 10 trillion bits per second down a single strand of fibre the diameter of a human hair – which is equivalent to almost 2,000 music CDs or 150 million phone calls every second.

On top of that, the PR industry is engaging with a blogosphere that is doubling in size every 200 days. More than 100 million YouTube video clips are being watched daily. And Google, the mother of all search engines, claims the revolution is just gathering pace. It says that five 'exabytes' of data are being added to the world's digital archives each year. One exabyte is equivalent to a megabyte – the capacity required to attach a single photograph to an email – followed by 18 zeros. Put another way, digital capacity equivalent to 41,000 years of television viewing is being added to the global online world, annually.

'Somewhere near the year 2020, you could have all the content ever created in a device that fits in the palm of your hand,' according to the chief executive of one global technology company.

As the technology arms race continues, companies and their PR advisers are trying to determine the impact of greater distribution and delivery speeds for information that they previously controlled tightly. The speed factor is particularly acute in automated share dealing. Automated algorithmic trading programmes – so-called 'algo-trades' – are just one example of how digital capabilities are transforming corporate interaction in which outside advisers might, previously, have played a role.

Clearly, there is not much room for investor relations guidance when an estimated 40 per cent of US share transactions are 'algo-trades' or when trading systems in London can process 4,200 orders a second.

Such trends have forced a rapid reassessment among PR companies of their digital capabilities. They have also opened the floodgates to a raft of new firms claiming specialist skills in managing technology or monitoring social media. In the marketing material typical of the new monitoring agencies, one firm promises to 're-engineer the news tracking and research market'. It adds, modestly: 'We achieve this through a combination of superior methodology, extensive data source and machine analysis, and first-rate consultancy-based human research. We selectively build proprietary technology to deliver integrated workflow support across operations – data collection, research production and publishing.'

All this verbiage disguises a rush for clients by firms hoping to capitalise on the digital anxieties of large companies. Those anxieties have grown with the rise of Twitter, blogs, Facebook, aggregation sites and old media masquerading as new media. For many companies this networked economy has led to a loss of control in corporate communications. It has reduced response times for potential problems, particularly when the media relies on search engines such as Google for news and background on a troubled business. The Google effect was summed up memorably by Ken Costa, the veteran investment banker, as 'knowledge long; wisdom short'. In other words, companies faced an environment where a huge audience could make assumptions based on scant, unverifiable, online data. But it raised the risk of poor judgments, a lack of accuracy and oversimplification.

In a bid to protect their reputations in an online world, numerous companies have stepped up media monitoring, launched their own Twitter accounts and embraced all manner of social networks. Hence, Royal Bank of Scotland used Twitter to try to quash media speculation around the 2011 bonus award to its chief executive, while Pearson turned to the same platform to deny media speculation that the *Financial Times* was for sale. But primarily, such corporate online strategies are focused on customer relationship management or pricing strategies rather than PR.

Before deciding how to communicate, companies are increasingly mining data from social networks in real time. Consultants at McKinsey found that companies including Ford, PepsiCo and Southwest Airlines were analysing consumer postings on social media sites including Facebook and Twitter to gauge the impact of their marketing campaigns and to understand how consumer sentiment about their brands is changing.

Such social media interaction can backfire on attempts to manipulate business reputations. Qantas, the Australian airline, suffered the consequences of clumsy online engagement when it asked its Twitter followers what they considered to be 'Qantas luxury', with inevitably racy responses. Tesco, the grocery retailer, had to fight off a Twitter and Facebook storm over its hiring practices after work experience roles were described as full-time positions. Such incidents demonstrate that social media is clumsy for some types of communication, serving to alienate rather than attract online followers. When eBay decided to issue its earnings on Twitter, it took four tweets just to cover the Securities and Exchange Commission (SEC) disclaimers – not a way to win digital friends.

While companies want to use digital tools, they too often fail to understand the rapidly shifting tides of social media sentiment. As a result, their digital efforts resemble the metaphorical 'granddad at the disco' – trying to dance but embarrassing themselves and their audience. This was certainly true during the first generation of online engagement, when companies were guilty of misusing blogs or online 'astroturfing': creating fake grassroots consumer campaigns to burnish their reputations. Executives have paid a particularly high price for getting it wrong with blogs.

The dangers of blogging were well illustrated by John Mackey, the chief executive of Whole Foods, the US company. He was investigated by regulators after posting anonymous posts about competitor Wild Oats Markets – a company that Whole Foods was bidding for. 'Anything I say or do is now at risk of showing up on the front page of a national daily newspaper, and therefore I need to be much more conscious about the implications of everything that I say or do in all situations,' he later wrote.[17]

One-dimensional corporate websites have also proved unsuitable for crisis situations, hard to modify and failing to meet audience demands for immediacy. Hence, in September 2008, the Merrill Lynch website was still proudly proclaiming 'Even in today's economy, there are always smart places for your money', on the same day that – in small print – the site published a small news item: 'Bank of America buys Merrill Lynch'. In the same month in Britain, HBOS also tried to bury similar news, publishing in a remote corner of its home page 'our latest news: HBOS confirms agreement to be acquired by Lloyds TSB'.

The searing experiences of mismanaging online announcements has persuaded companies to develop interactive, rich content sites that can be adapted quickly in response to a crisis or major developments. Many have also upgraded their monitoring capabilities to police so-called 'e-reputations'.

'It makes sense to take action and stop the rot,' says Luke Johnson, chairman of Risk Capital Partners, in *Business Life* for January 2012. 'Companies are increasingly using sophisticated software to scan the online world for negative tweets and then send direct messages to the individuals concerned in a bid to take the issues offline. In an age when bad news can go viral in an instant, eternal vigilance pays off.'

---

[17] http://www2.wholefoodsmarket.com/blogs/jmackey/2008/05/21/back-to-blogging

But the digital explosion is so rapid, and the megaphone tactics of some outlets so loud, that it is beyond companies or their advisers to address the sheer volume of traffic. BP suffered that fate during the Deepwater Horizon disaster, when traditional and digital media fed off each other in a vortex of alarmist criticism. In one example of digital distortion, the company was chastised online for 'deciding to wage chemical warfare' in the Gulf of Mexico. Bloggers spread fears of dispersant related diseases. 'It is commonly being called the Blue Flu, because the alleged symptoms include blue lips and skin, and it's scaring the hell out of people,' said one blogger. Another day during Deepwater Horizon, the digital airwaves were busy with allegations about 'Oil for Terrorism', claiming that BP was linked to pressuring the Scottish government to release the terrorist convicted for the Pan Am 103 bombing.

The shout-loudest approach of citizen journalism seeks to shock and awe various audiences. That poses acute problems for PR agencies seeking to manage client expectations. As the partner of one international agency says: 'While a relatively finite corps of print media was, up to a point, susceptible to a degree of management by a beleaguered corporate, it is much harder to manage the vast and sometimes venomous outpourings on the web.'

Citizen journalism, spanning individual blogs to aggregated community platforms, can be a major irritant. A much bigger threat is posed by organised digital activism targeting different institutions or corporations. Such direct action reached a peak in 2010 when the WikiLeaks website dumped hundreds of thousands of leaked files on to the web, allegedly trying to hold governments to account. When the targets of WikiLeaks' campaign sought to restrain publication, online supporters of the rogue service launched co-ordinated attacks on government institutions and leading corporations. Even other social networks were alarmed by the implications of WikiLeaks' offensive. 'Facebook took down a page used by WikiLeaks supporters to organize hacking attacks on the sites of companies [such as] PayPal and MasterCard,' according to Miguel Helft of the *New York Times* in the *International Herald Tribune* of 13 December 2010. 'Facebook said the page violated the terms of service, which prohibits material that is hateful, threatening, pornographic or incites violence or illegal acts.'

The WikiLeaks controversy has inflamed corporate wariness about digital exposure. That unease has been compounded by a wave of hacking action – often attributed to the online collective Anonymous – targeting companies including Sony and Intel. In such action, hackers usually use 'distributed denial-or-service' tactics, which swamp corporate sites with data until they crash. 'Anonymous is a handful of geniuses surrounded by a legion of idiots,' said Cole Stryker, an author who has researched the movement, in the *New York Times* on 4 March 2012. 'You have four or five guys who really know what they're doing and are able to pull off some of the more serious hacks, and then thousands of people spreading the word, or turning their computers over to participate in DDoS attacks.'

Reacting to such threats is beyond the capabilities of most PR advisers, even those who have invested heavily in digital services. Instead, firms are finding themselves participating in crisis-avoidance strategies with their clients, where cyber-security has become a major issue. For a company under digital attack, the PR advice is secondary to the security concerns over stolen information, compromised systems and so-called 'gateway protection'. Clients sense they can only start to rebuild their reputations once the digital attack is understood and under control.

Traditional PR advice in a digital crisis could be marginalised even further if companies' first reaction, when faced with a hacking assault, is to deploy automated systems with the ability to capture, compute, communicate and collaborate information. 'Embedded with sensors, actuators, and communications capabilities, such objects will soon be able to absorb and transmit information on a massive scale and, in some cases, to adapt and react to changes in the environment automatically,' according to researchers at McKinsey.

The explosive nature of digital distribution is forcing changes across the advisory sector. PR agencies, lawyers, brokers and investment bankers are all trying to adjust. All advisers have to restate their relevance in an environment where the sheer volume of online scrutiny is hard to monitor; one in which the need for security trumps old-style intermediation; and when response times in a crisis are reduced to minutes.

Some agencies have responded by claiming to be able to monitor not just traffic but influence online, and then to target opinion formers with tactical PR. That is easy to claim but harder to prove. Most corporates remain sceptical. And traditional agencies, a little fearful of the online world, try to argue that clients should focus on trusted media outlets – albeit in digital guise – to cut through all the white noise on the web.

The PR industry is at risk of polarisation between the evangelism of pure online players and the caution of the legacy firms. PR advisers are trying to support clients increasingly anxious about their reputations in a digital world, and in the absence of any industry consensus on how to manage opinions in the online ecosystem.

Faced with such uncertainty, PR executives need to be able to recognise the opportunities and challenges of the digital world, and to show they understand each new technology. But they also have to rely on their instincts about its limits. They need to be courageous enough to tell chairmen and chief executives, who are often caught in the headlights of the online juggernaut, when to ignore the digital static.

Given the evangelism of many digital gurus, it takes a brave adviser to indentify the limits of online engagement. But it seems clear that the web and the numerous devices used to access it are merely part of an evolving distribution platform – an alternative route to market for information. The old rules of advice on when and how to engage still apply, just in a different guise, and at different speeds. Advisers must be digitally literate, and able to help their clients understand the risk-benefits of online tools. 'What companies want is a digital early warning system and to be prepared; they don't expect PR firms to be engaging in hand-to-hand combat with bloggers,' says one leading online agency head.

Yet few agencies agree about digital services. There is no industry standard, much less a code of conduct. It means, as with traditional types of public relations, there is significant overpromise and under-delivery by agencies claiming online management skills. One thing is true: reputations are more precarious in a digital environment, where new tools are needed to protect companies. But using those tools can be dangerous in themselves, exposing agencies to the charge of trying to manipulate opinion in a world that champions transparency.

Careful digital engagement has merits. It offers clients a level of protection. But bungled engagement carries a higher price. It can make the client and its agency part of a damaging story about online deception. At worst, they may find themselves accused of laundering.

CHAPTER 12

The Launderette

Number 9, Grosvenor Square, London is a discreet building. There are no brass nameplates or corporate signage
on the white Georgian façade. This is home to Tony Blair
Associates (TBA), the strategic consultancy arm of the former
UK prime minister.

Inside, a pastel-shaded hallway leads into a series of sparsely
furnished sitting rooms. Officials talk discreetly about assignments and client identities that are kept confidential. Insiders
at TBA call it the department store. 'Each office represents a
different part of the world or a different function,' according to
one adviser familiar with the setup. 'On the ground floor, you
have Asia and good governance, upstairs it's the Middle East
and China. But no one knows what goes on at the top floor:
that's secret.'

From Grosvenor Square, a group of former political advisers, seconded bankers and foreign policy experts draft advice
for regimes seeking legitimacy. Mr Blair, who sees no conflict
with his role as the official envoy for the international Quartet
on the Middle East, has advised governments from Kuwait to
Kazakhstan on strategies to enhance economic progress.

His supporters argue that it is entirely legitimate for countries and corporations with a low or poor profile to better
explain their reform programmes in the mature political and
financial capitals of the world. Blair's critics accuse the former
prime minister of descending into dark arts. His international
consultancy, they claim, is a reputation launderette.

Many media observers now believe London has become the
international capital of 'reputation laundering', a trade that
promises PR makeovers for countries, political leaders or corporations in need of a glossy profile. 'It is increasingly common

for the capital's top public relations firms to work for dubious countries, rather than dodgy people,' says author and columnist Daniel Kalder in *The Spectator*, 5 November 2011:

> Many of these firms have nice, shiny, anodyne names – Chime plc, for instance, is headed by the former Number 10 adviser Lord Bell, and includes Zambia among its clients. Portland PR, run by Blair's former press secretary Tim Allan, advises the Kremlin on its dealings with the British government. Ambassadors are okay, it seems, but top London PR firms are better connected and more influential.

Strategic consultants and PR companies hate the term reputation laundering. They claim to be a force for good, helping little-known governments or businesses to establish links with opinion formers, political partners, potential investors and democratic institutions in countries such as the UK and the USA. Lord Bell, in particular, likens his business with foreign governments to the advocacy of a leading barrister. In effect, he argues that reputation management firms are doing an honest job for clients, whatever their background, who deserve to be clearly understood.

'We do communications work. If people want to communicate their argument we take the view that they are allowed to do so,' *The Guardian* reported Lord Bell saying on 4 August 2010. He repeated the claim of honest neutrality after the Arab Spring focused attention on the work of PR companies for regimes brought down by popular uprisings. Bell Pottinger attracted controversy following its client work for organisations such as the Egyptian Ministry of Information, the Economic Development Board of Bahrain and the governments of Belarus and Sri Lanka.

'No amount of media harassment or sensationalism is going to stop me representing clients that have a legitimate right to tell their story,' says Bell in the *Evening Standard* of 28 March 2011. 'There is a fad for attacking PR companies. There's everything to attack bankers, there's a thing to attack accountants. You just have to ride with the punches.'

The punches rained down even more heavily on Bell Pottinger at the end of 2011 after the London-based Bureau of Investigative Journalism targeted the agency. At the heart of the investigation, the firm was accused of telling executives representing the Uzbek cotton industry – in reality undercover journalists – that it could use its influence with Britain's ruling Conservative Party to enhance UK attitudes towards the former Soviet republic of Uzbekistan, thereby improving the country's international reputation. Bell denied the charge in a robust exchange with Jeremy Paxman on *Newsnight* in April 2012, and the agency has since been cleared of any wrongdoing by the Public Relations Consultants Association.

PR agencies and lobbyists have also been accused of misusing Wikipedia, the online reference encyclopaedia, to alter entries about clients, thus making Wikipedia the latest battleground between PR attempts to manage reputations on the one hand, and the internet's underlying commitment to greater disclosure and transparency on the other.

In early 2012 it was reported that Portland had made alterations to Wikipedia entries on behalf of its clients – a charge that was also levied at Bell Pottinger in 2011. Such incidents have raised debate about the PR industry's role in editing Wikipedia, whose founder Jimmy Wales has expressed frustration about conflicts of interest in such cases.

PR firms have been increasingly concerned about the accuracy of wikientries, which are often treated as fact by the sort of opinion formers they seek to influence. Journalists at the *Financial Times*, for example, increasingly depend on Wikipedia following the closure of the newspaper's editorial library and research service in a cost-cutting exercise some years ago. If *FT* reporters, regarded as Premier League targets by PR firms, use

Wikipedia for research, then naturally the PR industry would seek to put the best gloss on their clients' entries.

To the frustration of many, it is against the rules for advisers to re-edit Wiki references 'in order to promote your own interests or those of other individuals, companies or groups'.

Both Portland and Bell Pottinger insisted that they had never done anything illegal, and tried to play down the sense of anger in the wiki community. After meeting Wales, Lord Bell said, as reported in the *Financial Times* of 13 January 2012: 'We both agreed to make the system work better. It was clear that neither of us understood the system. What we were doing was being done by other agencies and what we did was nothing wrong.'

It should be no surprise to anyone that PR agencies may not play by the rules or take risks on behalf of their clients. This is nothing new. What has changed is the impact of electronic trails, which make it easier to discover how online profiles have been expertly cleansed. The events of 2010–12 just focused attention on how far agencies were prepared to go for dubious regimes.

The disputes over Wikipedia entries, or the controversy over Tony Blair Associates' client list, or the actions of firms that have represented variously the Kremlin, Chinese state institutions or other repressive regimes, have also highlighted the equivocal approach of many firms to the conduct and governance of their clients. And it has exposed the prime incentive for many of these firms – money.

In spite of PR agencies' grandiloquent claims that their main goal is to advance understanding of their clients' activities, it stretches credulity to imagine that they do so from a sense of duty. No one in the PR industry has taken a Hippocratic oath to help the information marketplace. The motivation is about fees and profitability.

If any organisation is willing to offer a multi-million dollar fee, it will be possible to find a communications agency ready and willing to fix their international reputation. Increasingly such fee-paying organisations are not industrial heavyweights seeking favourable media coverage or a bounce in their share prices. They have been overtaken by governments, privately owned companies and oligarchs as the highest payers.

The really big money is earned by agencies helping governments, for whom $20 million or $30 million is a negligible rounding error in their national budgets. Even supposedly impoverished countries and state-owned organisations seem ready to lavish spending on a good Western image. A few years ago the chairman of one leading international agency asked a PR colleague: 'What do you think of Hamas?' Once it was obvious that he was serious, his partner replied: 'You could work for them if you want but you might as well kiss goodbye to your US business.'

While regimes are ready to be generous for a better profile, listed companies are now more austere. Most businesses have fixed procurement processes and a duty to shareholders about overhead costs. There is a clear need to communicate effectively with outside audiences such as the media, regulators, investors and other stakeholders. The same budgetary constraints rarely apply to governments, particularly in those parts of the world where power is concentrated in one-party regimes, where the purse strings are held by a few individuals and where there is a significant appetite for Western approval.

The representatives of dubious governments or controversial unlisted corporations are more willing to pay a high price to see their reputations improved in leading capital markets. They are ready to do so because of the alien way – to their minds – in which the Western media behaves. In their home countries, state media, regulation and public opinion are frequently subject to tight controls. So they are naturally alarmed by the 'anything goes' marketplace of liberal democracies. And they are particularly exercised by unflattering commentary about their activities on the internet – all of which makes them potentially lucrative customers of the 'Launderette'.

For such clients, services range from those firms created specifically to enhance client reputations in a digital environment, and which are brazen about it, to mainstream PR agencies who order junior associates to secretly polish online references about their clients and remove unsavoury or allegedly inaccurate material. Many of these clients, who are unused to adversarial media engagement, dislike the 'front door approach' of simply talking to the media on a direct basis. Even though this obvious tactic often delivers reputational dividends, clients think the potential risks outweigh the benefits. In the metaphorical launderette, they do not want to hang out dirty washing in public. Indeed, many clients don't want to 'get their hands wet' at all. So they opt for dry cleaning.

In the reputation world, the dry cleaners are the often anonymous web specialists who promise to remove negative articles or damaging imagery from leading search engines. The *New York Times*, which has itself been the target of exposés about its journalistic standards, reported on 1 April 2011 that demand for online makeovers was supporting a new cottage industry of reputation managers. According to Michael Fertik, the chief executive of Reputation.com, a leading US search-enhancement company: 'We've reached a point where the Internet has become so complicated, vast and fast-paced, that people can't control it by themselves anymore. They now need an army of technologists to back them up online.'

Analysis by the *New York Times* found that most online reputation managers attempt to fool search engines. To trick the search engines, these managers employ programmers who create dummy websites that link their clients to a list of approved search results. The more links, the higher the approved sites rank. Numerous specialist firms have now opened their doors to clients desperate to repair their image or disguise unflattering digital reputations. They use sophisticated algorithms, automated response tools and linking systems to suppress uncomfortable coverage on the internet, or make it harder to find.

Attempts by agencies to manage opinion are nothing new. All that has changed is the sophistication of the digital devices and tactics at their disposal. The old practice of 'astroturfing', in which PR firms created fake grassroots campaigns to influence the media and other audiences, has simply moved into an online universe which is far harder to control. Organisations such as the American Petroleum Institute or the Council for Agricultural Science and Technology now boast sophisticated online capabilities to manage their target audiences. Like the PR agencies involved in such organisations, these groups proactively seek to advance their causes to build up a degree of reputation credit.

Such credit is invaluable when things go wrong, for no amount of laundering can protect a company when it is in the middle of a crisis. Efforts at reputation management by corporations such as BP, Goldman Sachs, News Corp or the Carnival cruise company that owned the ill-fated *Costa Concordia* – the huge ship which ran aground at Isola del Giglio in 2012 – proved fruitless while the full storm of public controversy was sweeping over the respective companies.

The tendency of clients and their advisers to apportion blame before the full facts were known made things worse for each organisation. No one with access to Western media believed claims by Arab governments that their insurgencies were the work of terrorists. Similarly, corporations have had to engage reverse gear after trying to escape full responsibility for their reputational meltdowns. BP damaged its own course by trying to blame Transocean initially for the Deepwater Horizon accident, just as Goldman Sachs pinned its responsibility for part of the financial crisis on rogue traders. News Corp likewise tried to blame a single rogue reporter for its hacking scandal in the UK. And Costa Cruises, the Carnival subsidiary, delivered a guilty verdict on its own ship captain for the disaster off the coast of Tuscany.

Commenting on Carnival's strategy, Nick Murray-Leslie, chief executive of Chatsworth Communications, said in

CorpComms magazine's February 2012 issue:

> Playing the blame game from the start was unacceptable
> when the crisis was still a crisis – prejudicial and unhelp-
> ful... The move to distance the Carnival brand name
> will backfire utterly. The strategy from the start was
> clearly to protect the parent by fronting with the Italian
> subsidiary, which in turn blamed the captain directly.
> This approach only works in the short term. The mas-
> ter brand will come under fire when the lawyers start
> getting busier.

The lesson of such crises is that reputation management theories are rarely effective when an organisation is in trauma. 'It
is clear that clients need to think about reputational risks in
peace time not war,' says one official involved in the BP crisis.
'There should have been much more rehearsing about how to
deal with the crisis. We didn't have a strategic message or disaster recovery plan that was ready to deploy in the right way, and
we had little reputational credit to fall back on in the US.'

Building and maintaining a positive reputation is not
easy. It is not a task that lends itself to manipulation, where
disclosure carries a very high price. If the laundering process involves digital manipulation tactics, or straightforward
subterfuge, clearly the reputational outcome will be the opposite of the one intended. Exposure can lead to a crisis of confidence in the advisory firm, a loss of clients and significant
brand damage.

It is no justification or defence to argue, as some advisers
have done, that they are simply acting in clients' interests in a
world without rules. Nor is there justification to claim that the
PR firm is the innocent messenger for a client who deserves a
hearing, whatever their past conduct. Such a defence falls away
when it becomes clear that the incentive for the messenger is
not born of vocational intent; it's just a matter of fees.

Faced with such allegations, and apparent evidence of misde-meanour, the PR industry and lobbyists may soon find them-selves in need of reputation management. And London may come to regret its status as the world's leading launderette.

CHAPTER 13

The Tower of Babel

Gershon Kekst has a framed letter on the wall of his office, high above Madison Avenue, signed by former US President Harry S. Truman. A scrawled handwritten note in the corner of the letter reads: 'Public relations cannot be learned except by experience.'

Kekst, the founder and chairman of the company named after him, is probably the most experienced business PR executive in New York. If Lord Bell is the poster boy for reputation management in London, then Gershon Kekst epitomises the professional services approach that defines the PR industry in North America.

When Enron was collapsing, its beleaguered communications officials turned to one agency: Kekst. Hollinger, the newspaper company and former publisher of the *Daily Telegraph*, called in the same firm to defend its reputation amid the fraud allegations swirling around Conrad Black, its disgraced former chairman. Kekst was also used by the Walt Disney Co. to protect its image when it was threatened by both a boardroom battle and a hostile takeover bid.

Given that corporate roll-call, the firm's founder is probably justified in saying: 'We are serious people inspired by serious work … we are determined; we are competitive. What energizes this firm in the best sense of the word is competitive striving.'

That sort of call to arms is echoed across the PR industry in the USA, which has evolved into a far more structured, codified, service proposition compared with its haphazard sister industry in the UK. The British style of business public relations was built around mercurial agency leaders, who depended on patronage and a Rolodex of useful contacts. The US system has long been a regulated market of firms with deeper industry experience, and an intake of PR school graduates with a closer affinity to the standards of professionalism of law firms.

The differences of approach and style on either side of the Atlantic reflect the wide international variety in the quality, codes of conduct, media experience and transparency of PR practices in different parts of the world. US leadership, when it comes to professional standards and the range of services, reflects the sheer size of its industry compared with all other PR markets.

According to the International Communications Consultancy Organisation (ICCO) *World Report 2011*, the fee income of PR firms in the USA reached €2.5 billion in 2010 – spread among 98 members of the US Council of Public Relations Firms. The UK was the second-largest market, with fee income of €872 million for the final year of the decade. The dominance of English-language markets in commanding PR fees was reflected by the fact that Australia ranked third in fee income at €304 million – almost the same total as the far larger economies of Germany, France and Italy combined.

The financial dominance of the US industry could be even larger given that Veronis Suhler Stevenson, the private equity firm which produces a respected communications industry forecast each year, believes that the American market for PR was worth $3.4 billion in 2010 – the last year for which figures are available.

The global fee variations are a useful indicator of different international maturity in the scope and sophistication of PR services. Taking four different markets – the USA, Germany, Japan and China – it is clear that the market and quality of advice that companies can expect ranges wildly from one country to the next. The USA emerges clearly as the most mature market.

By comparison, Germany is struggling to adjust with both an absence of large deal income and a relative lack of diversity in agency support. Corporations in Japan are still only now acknowledging the value of outside refugee communications support, which has restrained the evolution of its PR industry for many years. And China is trying to make a rapid transition from a state regulated media and business environment to a controlled capitalism model, in which PR agencies are beginning to play a larger and more lucrative role.

Identifying the trends supporting the US PR market, the ICCO said in its latest annual report, *World Report 2011*:

> Consumer communications helped grow the consultancy industry in the US, aided by increasing attention to social media and some regulatory changes from Washington – for example, the revised guidelines on online endorsements and testimonials, financial regulatory reform and new food and drug labelling directives. Healthcare, corporate and crisis communications further contributed to the growth of the business, while overall profitability of US consultancies improved.

Agency bosses in the USA argue that the continued growth is down to more than cyclical changes in demand. The relative size and health of the US market, they say, is a factor of the influence and professionalism of senior PR executives. 'We must operate at the same level in the C-suite as the general counsel; the operations manager; the chief marketing officer; and the director of corporate strategy. We are at exactly the moment in time when this is possible,' says Richard Edelman, the head of the eponymous US agency.

Mr Edelman, whose firm has more than 40 clients paying in excess of $1 million a year, on 10 November 2011 told the Institute of Public Relations in his address, 'Reimagining our Profession: Public Relations for a Complex World', that PR executives 'must help fashion operating strategies for companies and brands that transform the supply chain, propel innovation, motivate employees, and drive commercial success. We must also take a leadership role in creating the big idea that markets the strategy.'

Senior executives at other US agencies endorse that ambition. They say that the strength of the industry reflects the career choices of senior individuals who now opt for a communications career rather than other business professions. 'Today the people at the top of the PR business are regarded as well as people like the top of law firms or management consultants,' according to a partner at one firm with a leading American presence.

But there is no one-size-fits-all profile to the US market. It is heavily polarised. At one end of the spectrum there are full-service agencies such as Burson-Marsteller, Hill & Knowlton and Edelman, which boast very large client rosters, but whose margins are thin in mass market product communications. At the other end, there are specialist smaller agencies focused on only one industry such as technology or healthcare. They may compete, in turn, with firms dedicated to particular disciplines such as investor relations, financial communications or crisis work.

In-between the full-service firms and the specialist agencies, a group of mid-size international companies are fighting for business in a market that stretches from regular financial communications to mergers and acquisitions, major crises and executive reputation work. Firms including Kekst, Brunswick, RLM Finsbury, Glover Park and Sard Varbinnen are among those chasing business in this 'squeezed middle'.

Although the overall level of fees for the US market may be rising – up by 11 per cent in 2010 – all of these US firms are chasing project fee income against a background of downward pressure on retained monthly mandates. 'Crisis work has become vital because it gives you a cushion against the declining rates on annuity clients,' says a partner at one mid-tier firm in the USA. 'Crisis is the icing to keep your stars happy with bonuses. Retained work pays for the lights to be kept on.'

The level of payments for retainers or projects is decided invariably by the in-house head of communications, who in the

USA reports to the chief executive rather than the senior legal counsel, chief marketing officer or head of human resources. US PR advisers say that chief executives are taking a greater interest in PR fees and service delivery, reflecting their emerging responsibility as the cheap messenger for corporate strategy.

The involvement of chief executives in deciding US advisory fees, and in taking direct counsel from outside advisers, contrasts with a more conservative approach in most other countries – with the possible exception of the UK. In Germany, where 35 firms generate an estimated €180 million in annual fees, public relations leaders say the market is only just beginning to follow US trends towards holistic reputation management rather than specialist advisory roles in areas such as investor relations or product communications.

The managing partner of one German agency attributes the transition to increased corporate anxiety about media standards, and not due to a growing appetite for joined-up communications. 'There is a defensive reaction by German companies as the media itself changes because of the crisis in newspapers,' according to the executive. 'Business leaders are alarmed by German media outlets copying the campaign style journalism of *Der Spiegel*. News reporters are being replaced by investigative teams, and the business pages are being presented as entertainment.'

German media, nevertheless, remain less threatening than the adversarial approach in the UK or the USA. For set piece interviews, many news outlets still offer companies prior approval of questions and answers with their chief executives. But German agencies fear this will become the exception rather than the rule, and that Anglo-Saxon 'risk-taking' will begin to infect domestic journalism. As companies begin to share this anxiety it is having twin benefits for German firms: chief executives are increasingly ready to use outside advisers as communications confidantes, and they are willing to pay higher fee rates for the sort of advice they now receive at times of crisis.

If Germany is slowly gravitating towards the US model, it is doing so far more rapidly than the PR industry in Japan. This huge business marketplace does not have a tradition of mature expert agencies with long-standing relationships with leading companies. Where they are rethinking requirements, Japanese companies tend to use outside advisers mainly for product public relations.

John Sunley, president of Tokyo-based Ashton Communications, believes Japanese reticence about external advisers is changing amid a series of corporate crises and shareholder activism threats by foreign investors. But he warns that it will take some time to overcome corporate cultural resistance to taking advice from outsiders. 'Here in Japan, agencies are seen more along the US lines of professional services than the UK model of a wink and a nod. It would probably take overseas acquisitions to concentrate the minds of Japanese business leaders, but we haven't seen incoming deals so changes are slow,' says Sunley.

The modest appetite of Japanese corporates for Western style advisers partly reflects their conservative media engagement strategies. That tradition is dominated by Japan's press clubs, which were set up at the end of the Second World War by the Americans to ensure that all media got fair and equal access to news. Press clubs were established for every industry in Japan, and were often located in the headquarters of the biggest company in the sector.

'Japanese press clubs are designed to ensure that both sides – reporters and reported – played by a set of unofficial rules … In essence a form of self-regulation designed to avoid embarrassment and misunderstanding,' says Ian Hargreaves, Professor of Journalism at Cardiff University. 'To Western critics the style is, like other Japanese institutional practices, conservative, secretive and non-confrontational to the point where it represents a barrier to social and political progress.'[18]

---

[18] Ian Hargreaves, *Journalism: Truth or Dare?*, Oxford, Oxford University Press, 2003.

The impact of the internet and complaints by foreign media – excluded from the clubs – may yet erode the influence of the system. But the transition is moving at a snail's pace, partly because there is no tradition of disclosure by Japanese companies to external advisers. Strategic communications, moreover, has only recently been recognised as a dedicated career path. Hence the heads of communications at many Japanese companies are not PR specialists. Rather, they have been rotated through that department after spells as production managers, corporate strategists or chiefs of staff. Very few are women. PR in Japan is largely patriarchal. Given the different approach and culture of Anglo-American agencies, few firms have made significant inroads into the Japanese market, despite the large and significant number of companies requiring potential advice.

The slow pace of reform in Japan contrasts with rapid changes in China. Almost all of the leading US, UK and continental European agencies have set up offices or signed partnerships in China in the past ten years. More aggressive investment strategies by Chinese state institutions and a series of IPOs have created growing demand for world-class communications. Even so, agency executives in China say most of the revenue is not generated by Chinese companies seeking to improve their image at home. Instead, the PR business is dominated by mandates for foreign companies seeking to improve reputations in the world's second-largest economy, or by the out-bound traffic of large Chinese companies seeking to polish their image overseas.

'You have to have a regional model across Asia, encompassing China, to make real money in this country,' says one agency leader based in Beijing. Companies such as Burson-Marsteller, Ogilvy and Hill & Knowlton have done well with marketing consumer services, but the track record of financial PR houses has been far more mixed.

Part of the problem relates to a shortage of communications executives capable of advising companies investing into or from China. That problem is compounded by cultural differences over media engagement tactics. In China, for example, it is still common for agencies to pay reporters and media outlets for favourable coverage. The going rate for a flattering interview with the chief executive in Chinese media is about 7,000 renminbi. Companies and their agencies also pay 'taxi money' for reporters to attend the press conferences. The typical inducement for press conference attendance is 100 to 200 renminbi.

'Journalists are paid so badly in China that everyone complies with the taxi money culture,' says the president of one domestic PR agency. 'The bigger sums of money are paid for interviews and getting reporters to promise to write about your client.'

The culture gap in China extends beyond the tradition of low-level media corruption to a wide difference between what Chinese companies regard as effective media engagement, and how Western companies feel they are treated by Chinese business media. Chinese companies do not have the same sense of obligation as Western companies to provide proof points or justification for any news announcement they make. As a result, the senior management of companies from China are often frustrated at the lack of coverage internationally for press releases that are either contrived or anodyne – but which would normally be reported by their domestic media.

Conversely, international companies are surprised by the aggression of Chinese business reporters. While political commentary remains tightly controlled, the opposite is true when it comes to business news. In pursuit of a story, Chinese financial correspondents rarely abide by the rules of 'off-the-record' or background guidance. Many companies have found themselves embarrassed by discussions that they thought were not reportable, and which end up on front pages in China.

The evolution of the PR business in China and other emerging markets remains a far cry from the highly developed, financially robust and increasingly digital nature of the business in the world's largest market: the USA. The extreme variation between different territories has made it harder for international firms to roll out a single, consistent business model, or to apply a global set of fee arrangements and advisory services. Similarly, there are differences over traditional media engagement standards and the importance of social media.

In the USA, social media is seen as an embedded requirement for all agencies, given that they are already dealing with customers, employees, investors and regulators on a range of digital platforms. But the efficacy of such digital tools is far harder to measure in markets such as China, Russia or India. Almost 20 per cent of the firms questioned by the ICCO in its annual trends barometer said their clients do not see social media services as belonging to public relations at all.

In a comment reflecting both the digital and geographic divide in the industry, the ICCO said: 'Some dissonance exists between the offering and capabilities of PR consultancies and the views of the organisations they hope to serve. As demand for digital communications, and social media expertise in particular, continues to grow, it will be crucial for PR consultants to establish credibility in this area versus other marketing disciplines and specialists.'

The credibility of public relations is likely to continue to vary from market to market, reflecting the different rates of business maturity around the world. Some markets are regulated, populated by PR-trained graduates and subject to intense media scrutiny. Others, including the largely untapped territories of India and Russia, are years behind the Anglo-American model, frequently corrupt, potentially dangerous and the PR 'art' remains very dark. Yet, all companies have common anxieties – from media reporting standards to a fear of crisis. They are all vulnerable to criticism about strategy, remuneration, product reliability or financial performance. International clients are all worried about the shape of the global economy and the future security of their businesses. So it is a frustration to many of them that they can't get consistent advice on how to address such challenges.

Achieving a global industry standard in public relations has so far proved elusive. But it is a goal worth pursuing. Whether in Beijing, Tokyo, Frankfurt or New York, Gershon Kekst probably speaks for the future of the whole industry when he says: 'The role of the strategic communications consulting firm is to provide an independent perspective to its clients and business leaders to help them understand how to achieve a redefinition of their companies in a fast paced, changing environment. Nothing could be more timely or more urgent.'[19]

---

[19] 'Inside Kekst', www.kekst.com

CHAPTER 14

Intelligence Agencies

Boardroom disquiet at the variable nature of international PR has persuaded more companies to consider alternative measures to protect their hard-won reputations

A small army of advisory businesses has sprung up, offering industry intelligence, strategic communications services and crisis avoidance tools to different industrial groups. In recent years, traditional PR firms have found themselves in competition with boutique financial businesses, specialist legal counsel and private security agencies – all vying for the ears of the chairmen and chief executives. A combination of boardroom anxiety over reputational damage and a rapid demarcation of advisory roles has allowed new players to encroach on the marketplace previously monopolised by senior PR executives.

This business incursion has been particularly lucrative for the self-styled 'intelligence agencies'.

Occupying a grey area between private detectives and forensic accountants, these secretive companies have won significant amounts of business from clients looking for market intelligence to help shape or protect their core strategies.

The success of these firms is due partly to the collective paranoia of large corporations, many of whom have a heightened sense of reputational risk following the defenestration of famous companies including BP and News Corp. Having seen PR activities fail to contain the brand damage for such businesses, the chief risk officers or audit committees of large companies have begun to allocate significant sums to consultancies offering useful risk analysis and industry intelligence.

This is creating a new competitive market between PR firms, which are trying increasingly to sell reputation protection services, and a growing number of security companies that are migrating from military capabilities to risk management advice and strategic communications.

On one side of this marketplace, the PR firms offer proven media handling skills and the ability to shape coverage on behalf of their clients. On the other side, the intelligence agencies promise better strategic risk analysis and crisis avoidance capabilities. In theory, the two disciplines should co-exist happily. The firms at the security end of the spectrum – often staffed by former army officers, CIA and MI6 agents – tend to work below the radar. They do not engage with the media or proactively manage reputations with external audiences. Their activities are largely 'upstream', gathering information and analysis for executives to determine strategy, while most PR firms are focused 'downstream' on communicating those strategies once they have been decided.

But in practice, corporate intelligence and PR companies are converging in the 'mid-stream', where they meet each other across the boardroom table – each offering competing advice to senior management. The leaders of firms from both sides of the market aspire to 'consigliere' status with the chairmen or chief executives of their client companies. The increasing influence and capabilities of the intelligence agencies poses a new competitive threat to PR agencies that are already struggling to assert their relevance in a world of corporate crises, fragmenting media and shrinking budgets.

Companies on either side of the advisory community would argue that they occupy different roles for their corporate clients. There are certainly significant differences in the pedigree and operating culture of the PR and intelligence agency players.

Most leaders in the international PR community hail from a background rooted in marketing, investor relations, journalism or brand management. Their counterparts in private intelligence usually migrate into the corporate world from the armed services or national security agencies.

Mike Baker, Nick Day and Tim Spicer are typical of the intelligence veterans who have adapted their 'Cold War' experience for commercial gain. Baker and Day, respectively former officers with the Central Intelligence Agency in the USA and the UK's MI5 intelligence service, are the founders of Diligence, a US–UK business specialising – among other things – in reputational threats and risk management. Diligence, which acts for about 300 clients around the world, says it uses research and analysis to deliver 'the "information edge" required for success in an era of unprecedented global competition and risk'.

Similar claims are made by Aegis, one of the UK's largest private security and intelligence firms. It was founded by Lt Col Spicer – after 20 years in the armed services – with a pledge to 'offer the best possible human intelligence and risk mitigation advice'. The mission statements of such companies are derived clearly from their former employers, such as the CIA, which defines part of its role as collecting information for 'key intelligence consumers [to] help them meet their needs as they face the issues of the post-Cold War world'.

In the converging world of risk management, this sort of language is also being adopted by PR firms, which talk of increased hostility and threats to corporate reputations. The overlap and potential duplication is clear from some of the statements issued on either side of the advisory community. Alan Parker, the founder and chairman of Brunswick, in the *Brunswick Review* of winter 2010, says:

> Trust is at the heart of any strong relationship, personal or corporate, and communication is at the heart of building and maintaining trust. Organizations of every kind are increasingly being challenged on why they should be trusted, by the media, investors, regulators, governments and employees who are naturally casting a more critical eye over what the company's management said it is going to do, and what it is actually doing.

His comments echo those of Nick Day, who runs the UK arm of Diligence. Commenting on his clients' appetite for risk management advice, in the *Wall Street Journal* of 22 June 2010, Day says:

> Increasingly what we find is that we will go and meet the chairman or chief executive of a corporation and they will say 'I absolutely trust my employees but they are inclined to tell me what they think I should hear.' Actually what they [the CEOs] are really looking for is the truth. In many cases they want someone to give a non-emotional, non-partisan view of what is happening in a particular scenario.

Similar pledges of 'strategic advice in an increasingly complex and unpredictable world' illustrate the common ground occupied by PR firms and intelligence agencies that include G3 Good Governance Group, Risk Advisory, Montrose, Guidepost Solutions and Stirling Assynt among others. Their service offerings – ranging from transactional support, dispute resolution and regulatory compliance to competitor analysis and advice on communication strategy – are causing some anxiety for PR firms which thought such skills were their core competence.

The overlap reflects a pursuit of legitimacy from different ends of the advisory landscape. PR firms are stressing reputation management and risk analysis because clients are less willing to pay for commoditised press release distribution or financial calendar work. The security agencies, by comparison, are sometimes trying to escape a legacy of quasi-military operations.

Aegis, for example, is a major provider of armed private security services in conflict zones such as Afghanistan and Iraq. The controversy over such activities and an increasing threat of regulation is persuading more players in the security field to build advisory capabilities for large corporate clients.

Lt Col Spicer's business is part of a wider migration. Aegis aims to utilise its security experience in countries such as Iraq, where it has more than 1,500 staff, to win advisory mandates – particularly in the energy sector. Boasting a strong focus on oil and gas, the firm says on its website:

> Our support services include market research, due diligence, political and reputational risk assessment, personality profiling, influence mapping, identification of legal and regulatory obstacles, and guidance on religious, tribal and regional affairs ... We have fostered excellent relationships with Iraqi ministries and national oil companies, are the security and intelligence provider to several international oil companies and their partners, and provide support in most other key sectors.'[20]

While PR firms would recognise the terminology of 'reputational risk assessment' and so-called 'influence mapping', their idea of protection is far removed from the definition adopted by security firms such as Aegis. Unlike PR, Spicer's outfit provides clients with a code of conduct covering 'use of force'.

The company says: 'Although Aegis operations are protective, personnel often work in unstable and violent environments which necessitate the carriage of firearms. When Aegis personnel are armed, they carry arms for personal protection, or the protection of those in their care, or to protect the innocent.'[21] In the Aegis 'Code of Conduct', ironically, the use-of-force rules are listed immediately after its pledge on corporate social responsibility, in which it promises 'to undertake all its projects in a socially responsible way'.

Such codes of conduct are an exercise in reassuring potential clients that they will not be embarrassed by doing business with self-styled strategic risk specialists – thereby opening up new revenue streams and diversification opportunities for

---

[20] 'Aegis Advisory in Iraq', 2011, www.aegisworld.com
[21] 'Aegis Code of Conduct', 2010, www.aegisworld.com

such firms. Their ability to secure risk assessment mandates also reflects the heightened sensitivity among large corporations about potential crises, many of them arising out of unforeseen compliance issues, unwanted media scrutiny or reputational threats in far-flung overseas operations.

The Arab Spring of 2011 and Middle East turmoil of 2012 have prompted several large companies to seek risk management advice about how their dealings with different regimes could adversely affect their global reputations. BP, for example, was alarmed during the Deepwater Horizon oil spill disaster to find itself under scrutiny for dealings with Libya, which Fox News, the polemical TV broadcaster, headlined 'Oil for Terrorism'. Another European company saw its reputation threatened following the exposure of historic engineering equipment sales to Iran. A third blue-chip company recently called in the risk advisers amid concern that infrastructure contracts in Syria could hamper its ability to do business in the USA.

Such cases, where companies seek both industry intelligence and PR reassurance, have increased following the US Justice Department's intensifying campaign against alleged corporate bribery and corruption. 'At least 78 corporations [have faced] investigation for possible violations of the foreign corrupt practices act, a 35-year-old law that bans American companies from paying bribes to government officials abroad. Among those companies are such well-known names as Alcoa, Avon, Goldman Sachs, Hewlett-Packard, Pfizer and Wal-Mart stores, although none of these companies have been charged,' according to the *New York Times* of 18 March 2012. 'And it recently emerged that News Corporation, which is controlled by Rupert Murdoch and has been trying to contain the damage from a phone-hacking scandal in Britain, is the subject of an FBI inquiry into possible bribery there and in Russia.'

This climate of fear is persuading even companies certain that they will be vindicated of any wrongdoing to seek outside counsel about how to minimise their reputational exposure.

Among the various advisers offering help, most large PR firms like to think they can compete effectively in providing risk-measurement strategies and mitigation tactics. But they are now increasingly finding themselves competing for business with companies, such as Aegis of the UK or Guidepost Solutions in the USA, which have links to national security agencies and the intelligence community that few public relations executives can match.

Describing one such mandate, Aegis says it was asked to investigate the circumstances of an asset seizure in the former Soviet Union and to draft a strategy for its return. 'Using source networks in four countries, we mapped the links between key government officials and local managers in the affected entity, identifying individuals who had driven the seizure and the decision-makers who had supported the process administratively,' according to the firm. 'From this, we were able to rebalance our client's efforts from the courts to a structured engagement with the appropriate figures of influence.'[22]

This sort of capability puts most PR firms at a disadvantage. They simply do not have the intelligence execution capability to put some of their risk management recommendations into action. Nevertheless, the PR players have a measure of protection from the encroaching services of the intelligence or security firms, simply because of their determination to remain behind the scenes. Discretion and confidentiality are basic principles for companies such as Risk Advisory, Aegis and Diligence.

These firms treasure their secrecy and find it extremely uncomfortable when they become part of a media story. One of the most secretive firms, Hakluyt, found itself caught up in 2012 in the controversy over the death of Neil Heywood, a British business consultant linked to Bo Xilai, the purged Communist Party secretary in the Chinese city of Chongqing.

---

[22] www.aegisworld.com

UK newspapers suggested Heywood was a consultant to Hakluyt, formed by MI6 and former military officers in the 1990s. 'It has not been pleased by these latest reports of its involvement in the "murky world of corporate intelligence" and has been keen to play down Heywood's role,' reported the *Daily Telegraph* on 31 March 2012.

As long as they have a deep aversion to media scrutiny or engagement, the intelligence firms will ensure that their PR competitors will secure advisory mandates about how to communicate externally and how to limit the reputational damage once a crisis becomes public over alleged corruption, abuse of sanctions policies or other sorts of misconduct.

In the case of News Corp's phone-hacking scandal in the UK, for example, the role of the forensic auditors and legal teams trawling through more than 300 million emails has been clearly ring fenced from the work of the PR agencies seeking to protect the company's reputation. One PR adviser involved with News Corp says its role had nothing to do with defending the allegations at the heart of the scandal: 'Our sole purpose was to restore the companies licensed to operate.'

Questions about the legality and intelligence gathering tactics by private security firms – whether real or imagined – have been a major incentive for businesses in the intelligence arena to move into the mainstream strategic advisory sector. The pursuit of a cleaner image has encouraged such firms to redefine themselves as reputation risk managers with a growing capability in strategic communications. This, in turn, has brought the intelligence end of the advisory market into direct competition with PR advisers seeking a greater slice of the action in advising boards on crisis management and avoidance techniques.

For the moment, PR agencies and their intelligence counterparts are managing to co-exist even if their reputation management services overlap. Yet over time, the similarities in their services could lead to consolidation or partnerships. The impetus for such tie-ups will escalate if clients tire of different advisers trying to sell increasingly duplicative services, which could be exacerbated by other players such as law firms, management consultants and investment bankers all claiming strategic communications skills.

Given that level of potential competition, PR firms have little room for complacency. Among the intelligence agencies, Diligence – which takes pride in its CIA and MI5 heritage – maintains that the determinants of success in an increasingly crowded market will be simple. It says: 'We believe that, in business, whoever has the best people wins.'

CHAPTER 15

Talent Pool

Each year, the leaders of the world's largest PR agencies convene their senior management for closed-door 'away days', where they review strategy, growth targets and the range of people working for their respective firms.

The away days take place in the ballroom of a grand hotel, usually in a city that is either a seat of government or home to important clients. Guest speakers from high finance or political office address the assembled partners, educating the generously paid audience about macroeconomic trends, election prospects, the latest compliance issues and the difficulties of assembling the right team to realise the company's ambitions.

At some point in the proceedings – most likely the opening or closing ceremony – the PR firm's founder or parent group's chief executive will opine about the major challenges and opportunities ahead. In a typical sermon to PR partners, the founder of one agency recently told his senior team: 'We have to become better relationship managers and we must train our people how to look after clients. And we must ask ourselves how do we keep our best talent? Of course, we should not take anyone on unless they are outstanding. But if we lose our hunter culture – for both clients and for talent – if we lose that edge, we are finished.'

These annual exhortations are replicated at almost all professional services firms, where the main operating assets are their people. The success of a PR firm, or any other advisory business, depends on a workforce that must combine integrity, influence, quality communication skills and the ability to persuade clients that they are trustworthy.

But unlike most professions public relations has no standard career path. There is no obvious ladder to climb. There are no parallels, for example, with the British legal system whereby a graduate ascends through bar school to pupillage to a place in chambers to senior counsel, before becoming a QC and eventually sitting on the judges' bench. Instead, the senior ranks of the PR industry are populated by corporate nomads, a tribe drawn from marketing, financial services, politics, the law, diplomacy, the media and occasionally pure PR men who have known no other trade.

Trying to manage such a collection of individuals is an exercise in public relations in itself. Executives of such varied pedigree do not, naturally, lend themselves to teamwork. They are notoriously protective of their business contacts and territorial about their client relationships. The self-preservation instincts of PR executives are particularly acute in firms where each industry team is treated as a stand-alone profit centre, and rewarded each year according to the revenues they generate. Even in firms that claim to be single profit centres there is suspicion among the partners and between different offices about who is up and who is down – a speculation game that intensifies with each annual bonus season.

The chairman of one large PR firm compares managing his partners to herding cats, describing it as the single biggest challenge he faces. Unwilling to poison the atmosphere at his international agency, he declines to comment directly about the individuals whose avarice or political manoeuvring make life difficult. Instead he cites an inspired speech by Sir Ove Arup, chairman of the consulting engineering group bearing his name, that was made in July 1970 but which still resonates today. In it, Sir Ove highlighted quality staff as a vital component of success:

> Presumably a good man comes to us in the first instance because he likes the work we do, and shares or is converted to our philosophy. If he doesn't he is not much good to us anyhow. He is not mainly attracted by the

salary we can offer, although that is of course an important point – but by the opportunity to do interesting and
rewarding work, where he can use his creative ability, be
fully extended, can grow and be given responsibility ...

If he finds after a while that he is frustrated by red tape
or by having someone breathing down his neck, someone for whom he has scant respect, if he has little influence on decisions which affect his work and which he
may not agree with, then he will pack up and go. And so
he should. It is up to us, therefore, to create an organisation which will allow gifted individuals to unfold.

For most of its history, the PR sector has not offered a structured
career environment that nurtured individuals. At a senior level,
executives tended to drift into public relations from other occu-
pations that they found insufficiently interesting or rewarding.
Lower down the ranks, junior associates often ended up in PR
after initially pursuing more glamorous paths in industries as
diverse as stockbroking, advertising, management consultancy
or the media.

But in recent years, PR has begun to gain traction, in mature
markets, as a career destination in its own right. A growing
number of graduates – especially from English-speaking markets – are applying to join agencies having either studied public
relations as a degree course or having been advised by their
career tutors that it is an industry receptive to their liberal
arts or social science education. Hundreds of US colleges
and schools now churn out PR students; all tutored in mul-
timedia communications skills. The University of Southern
California, the University of Texas and Syracuse University
rank as the top three best colleges for public relations in North
America, most boasting their own student-run PR agencies and
courses dedicated to government, corporate, consumer and
economic communications.

From Arizona to Wisconsin, the plethora of American college courses in PR is being matched by the expansion of similar programmes in the UK. Some 40 colleges in Britain now offer PR degrees, with the University of Sunderland alone offering more than 90 PR-related courses including public relations with psychology, with criminology and even with drama. In the Department of Culture prospectus for 2012, the joint honours PR–drama degree claims that

> public relations is a fascinating and exciting media related industry where careers can take many directions; some people in public relations are linked to celebrities, working to enhance their reputations and to guide them through times of crisis … The drama curriculum is designed to enable students to explore the interplay between practical performance skills and knowledge of the traditions of the subject.

The breadth of these courses is rarely matched by in-house training in the PR industry. Senior agency executives rarely have the time or the inclination to tutor new graduates on their first step of the career ladder. So entry-level associates are often left with menial but important chores such as media monitoring or pressing the 'send button' for a press release which they have had no hand in crafting. In a blog post for *Harvard Business Review* on 19 January 2012, industry commentator Alex Goldfayn said the work was thankless and generally unrewarding. 'A high failure rate is common and expected,' he added. 'This is why most media relations people are young, recently out of college, and generally unsophisticated. It's why most PR people move jobs frequently, looking for something better.'

That indictment is confirmed by young members of the PR diaspora who have left the industry in frustration. 'The biggest problem was a lack of structure or even support functions that one expects in a big professional services company,' says one junior executive who quit a leading agency for a career in management consulting. Another escapee complains: 'No one knew how the promotions system worked in PR. It seemed opaque, and sometimes based on nothing more than the last piece of work you complete. In the end it just grinds you down.'

The rate of churn and variable skills among young PR practitioners is a matter of concern in both mature and emerging markets. 'The US and UK report a general shortage of candidates with both digital expertise and client service experience,' according to the International Communications Consultancy Organisation (ICCO) *World Report 2011.* 'Switzerland suffers from a lack of highly experienced, senior talent. Brazil and India lack qualified workers for entry-level positions. In India, this is exacerbated by the fact that new candidates are drawn to advertising and existing staff leave for corporate positions since both of these offer better pay than PR consultancies.'

In its latest annual report, the organisation warned that the issue of attracting talent and retaining it was one of five major challenges facing the entire industry, alongside shrinking client budgets, margin pressure on fees, downward pricing by new or low-end competitors and increasing competition from new consultancies and other marketing disciplines.

Richard Edelman, head of the world's largest independent PR firm – employing 3,200 staff, agrees that attracting and developing talent with broad skills is one of the most urgent challenges facing the industry. Edelman needs a steady supply of qualified professionals to sustain its annual revenues of around $700 million, generated from 54 offices worldwide. The US-based company, which acts for clients including Microsoft, Unilever, AstraZeneca, Samsonite and Swiss Re, believes that undergraduate PR curriculums are not equipping new executives with the most relevant skills. 'Future practitioners should be required to take basic courses in economics, engineering, finance, foreign language[s], government, and statistics,' Edelman argued in 'Reimagining PR in the Age of

Complexity', his address to the Institute of Public Relations on 10 November 2011:

> This last course is essential as we must use new insight tools to find digital influencers and rigorously measure our results across all stakeholder groups.
>
> And once in business, practitioners should be given the opportunity for line experience, time overseas, and exposure to the public sector ... PR must offer a career, not just a first stop. We have to look hard at the salaries we are offering – starting at the junior level. And we have to welcome professionals from the other disciplines along the policy–communications continuum.

The variable standards of training and career development in PR have become an industry-wide problem because most agencies have been focused primarily on winning and preserving fee income from clients, most of whom rely on highly experienced advisers. Those senior advisers have a sense of ownership about their clients, and do not readily share their business-winning secrets. That model works well if the client handler is not overstretched. But if they are juggling too many relationships then client dissatisfaction is inevitable, especially if untrained junior executives are left to pick up the pieces.

In a revealing survey of corporate sentiment about UK public relations, more than 40 per cent of in-house communications directors expressed disappointment with the quality of advice that they received. A large proportion also complained about the level of fees they were charged, and 12 per cent of those questioned said that, while senior agency directors pitched for the business, they were left with 'junior-level service at senior-level fees'. The survey, conducted in the UK by *CorpComms* magazine and published in February 2012, quoted one in-house director of communications describing this as 'the typical structure of the industry; it is seriously flawed. The industry is ripe for some serious disruption'.

Such threats and client discontent have encouraged more agencies to improve their training programmes, with some forging partnerships with universities to nurture PR executives of the future. But these efforts are often ad hoc, involving theory-based courses in subjects such as accounting without relevant client-facing experience.

The hit and miss approach to career development in PR agencies contrasts sharply with an increasingly codified structure of management training in the client companies they serve. Directors of corporate affairs are increasingly sent away for intensive training at institutions such as Harvard or Insead, where they are encouraged to share ideas about entrepreneurialism and team work. 'The aim is to turn spin doctors into managers; people who can run large, complex communications departments rather than just engage on a one-to-one basis with the media,' says the director of human resources at a leading European corporation.

Management capabilities in corporate communications have become far more important given the rapid expansion of such departments as companies increasingly in-source their media relations, rather than relying on outside agencies. The growing sophistication of in-house resources includes multi-media capabilities and even digital newsrooms, which prepare executive interviews and pre-packaged news videos for distribution to the media.

Senior management is now demanding analysis and data from their media departments that outside agencies often struggle to provide. 'Directors no longer value clippings services; they want decision-ready data that enables them to react quickly around potential crises or seize opportunities as they arise,' according to a director of strategy at one blue-chip firm. 'For too long there has been conspicuous absence of data tracking skills and analysis in communications.'

Large corporations are, therefore, investing significant sums in building in-house capabilities, attracting better qualified communications leaders to departments previously seen as ancillary to the core operation. The upgrade in skills and experience has been underway at some companies for years, starting with strategy, investor relations, legal counsel and now communications.

Jack Welch, the iconic former chairman of General Electric, argues that the transformation in such departmental capabilities began a generation ago when GE picked young high-potential financial managers with marketing zeal to overhaul investor relations.

'Each one of them became the chief marketing officer for GE stock, constantly on the road visiting investors and selling GE's story,' writes Welch. 'The job went from defensive line backer to offensive halfback … Already on a fast track because of their financial acumen, they used the job to improve their sales and presentation skills. The position went from a dead-end assignment to one of the most sought-after. It became a terrific training ground.'[23]

The gap emerging between the structured management development programmes for in-house communications roles and the slightly haphazard structure of agency training creates a potential hazard for the PR providers. Agencies do not want to duplicate in-house capabilities, which are inevitably better resourced, but nor do they want to admit to any shortcomings in service provision.

At a time when all PR firms are chasing fees and trying to contain overheads, it is hard to justify significant investment in skills training for junior staff when clients are demanding greater access to senior partners, whose counsel they value and trust. But without nurturing and developing junior talent, agencies will struggle to generate creative ideas for their clients, particularly in a fast changing digital environment that most middle-aged PR managers struggle to understand. In a vicious

---

[23] Jack Welch, *Jack: What I've Learned Leading a Great Company and Great People*, London, Headline, 2001.

circle, those firms that compromise or lose their reputation for promoting rising stars will cease to be on the application list for the brightest and best people joining industry. In turn, agencies that fail to replenish or refresh their executive talent will find it increasingly hard to preserve their own reputations for service excellence.

Given that human resources are the main asset of any PR company – it is a false economy to economise on skills training or career development. The trend displayed by large clients to in-source communication functions and instigate a general downward pressure on fees makes significant investment in people harder to justify. But failure to do so will inevitably compromise the reputation of PR firms, whose stock in trade is supposed to be reputation management.

The chairman of the British Institute of Directors (IoD), Neville Bain, summed up the dilemma in a guidance document for PR consultants and board directors, 'Reputation and the Board', issued in 2011 by the Chartered Institute of Public Relations. 'Firms with strong positive reputations attract better people. This gives rise to a virtuous circle of greater efficiency, better relationships with customers and suppliers, and enhancement of legitimacy in the eyes of society as a whole,' said the IoD. 'In the absence of a good reputation, the ability of the company to create value is severely impaired.'

The impairment threat to business reputations has escalated since the financial crisis that erupted in 2008 and has been punctuated since then by a well-publicised series of corporate crises. The quality and depth of PR staff available to deal with such threats has been adversely affected by the industry's poor track record in developing and retaining top talent. The challenge for the period ahead is clear. The PR industry needs to develop a structured career path that attracts creative talent from both higher education and rival business areas. Its senior leadership needs to invest more money and time in nurturing the executives who will one day replace them. Client trust needs to be rebuilt in the quality of up and coming junior staff. Agency leaders should avoid juggling clients, learning instead to share them with fully qualified colleagues. Only by doing so will the PR industry have a better chance of managing its own reputation over the next cycle.

CHAPTER 16

Quadrennial Test

In global public relations, the business cycle tends to follows 'the quadrennial' – the four-year tracking measure for marketing and communications spending.

Each quadrennial is dominated by a series of global events that drive investment in marketing, advertising, communications and PR: the Olympic Games, US presidential elections and the European football championship. The last quadrennial year, 2008, saw record billings, revenues and profits for the world's advertising and marketing services industry.

Since then, worldwide spending on public relations has continued to rise – from $7.45 billion in the year of the Beijing games and Barack Obama's election victory to $10.2 billion in 2011 – with a further increase anticipated for the 2012 quadrennial year.

Sir Martin Sorrell, chief executive of the marketing services giant WPP, argues that spending habits in public relations and other marketing services have been impacted by a profound change in corporate behaviour. Writing in the company's 2011 annual report, he warned:

> Ever is a long time, but I am not sure corporates will ever behave in the way they did before 2009. US-based multinationals are sitting on cash balances of as much as $2 trillion, with relatively unleveraged balance sheets. Boards remain unwilling to take excessive risks. External governance pressures are so intense and non-executive rewards are so slim, it is not really worth it. With the average chief executive lasting about four and a half years in the US and the average chief marketing officer only two, why take a big chance?

In spite of the risk-averse sentiment at the top of many large companies, spending on marketing services include PR has continued. Overall spending on communications services increased to almost $840 billion in 2011, up from $760 billion at the beginning of the quadrennial cycle. But PR expenditure still remains the smallest component of that total, lagging behind advertising, direct and specialist communications, sponsorship and market research. More worrying for the PR industry, spending in the mature markets of Europe and North America has remained largely flat at $2.3 billion and $3.9 billion, respectively, over the last cycle. Almost all the growth has come from Asia-Pacific activity, where investment in PR increased more than threefold to $3.5 billion in 2011, according to figures compiled by the WPP subsidiary GroupM.

As a result, the four-year quadrennial between 2008 and 2012, characterised by flat-lining European and US expenditure, has been a period of turmoil in business and financial public relations. A difficult cycle that began with the credit crisis has been compounded by PR traumas at an unprecedented number of iconic companies. Those troubled companies have been flailed, in turn, by a business media community fighting for its own survival in the face of a digital revolution in content, distribution systems and devices.

Structural change in media and communications has coincided – during the quadrennial – with a cyclical upturn in crises and increased pressure on business leaders from shareholders, regulators and politicians. Those pressures have reduced job security in senior management, creating a further major challenge for PR advisers having to explain the revolving door among senior executives. 'Over the past decade turnover among Fortune 500 CEOs has increased significantly; the average tenure has fallen from nine years or so to about four,' says A.G. Lafley, former chief executive and chairman of Procter & Gamble, in the *Harvard Business Review* of January 2011. 'And companies are increasingly turning to outside "saviors" because they are dissatisfied with internal candidates. Look at Hewlett-Packard. It recently hired an outside CEO for the third time in 10 years, creating a lot of drama and controversy. The on-going failure to develop a succession plan that includes viable internal candidates reflects poorly on HP's call and on HP's CEO.'

Companies from Air France to Bertelsmann, eBay, GM, Lloyds TSB, Nokia, NBC Universal, RIM, Sony, Toyota and Yahoo! – among many others – are all ending the four-year quadrennial with different leaders from those they started with. Companies that have held on to their chief executives have not escaped media criticism either, particularly if their leadership team has been accused of overseeing corporate misconduct.

Goldman Sachs is a typical target of the anti-business mood characterising the current era. It has found itself in the media's crosshairs at both ends of the cycle. In 2008, the investment bank was roundly criticised by the US Congress over its 'big short' against the American mortgage market. And in 2012 its reputation was shredded again when Greg Smith, a London-based Goldman's banker, went public in the *New York Times* of 14 March with a resignation broadside accusing his employer of ripping off clients. 'When the history books are written about Goldman Sachs, they may reflect that the current chief executive officer, Lloyd C. Blankfein, and the president, Gary D. Cohn, lost hold of the firm's culture on their watch,' wrote Smith. 'I truly believe that this decline in the firm's moral fiber represents the single most serious threat to its long-run survival.'

Other iconic names have struggled to reassert their reputations throughout the quadrennial. Back in 2008, BP was trying to rebuild morale following the sudden departure, the year before, of its chief executive Lord Browne. Two years later, it was brought to its knees by the Deepwater Horizon oil spill disaster, and was still facing multi-billion dollar compensation claims and questions over its long-term strategy deep into 2012.

Similarly, the scandal at News Corp over alleged phone-hacking at its UK newspaper subsidiary has festered since 2008 and developed into a full blown reputational crisis for the Murdoch-controlled media empire. The saga has led to multiple resignations at the company and disrupted the assumed ascendancy of James Murdoch as his father's successor. Their reputations were badly damaged by a controversial UK parliamentary report in May 2012, which concluded that Rupert Murdoch was 'not a fit person to exercise stewardship of a major international company', while his son James was guilty of 'wilful ignorance' about the extent of wrongdoing at News International.

Over the course of the quadrennial, such corporate misdemeanours have coincided with a loss of confidence in the wider global economy. Public relations and public affairs companies of all types will struggle to project positive messages for their clients against a backdrop of lingering macro-uncertainty and political austerity measures. Kenneth Rogoff, professor of economics at Harvard University, describes the problem as a 'credibility deficit', reflecting the failure of both governments and corporations to come to grips with the long, slow growth period that is typical of a post-financial crisis recovery.

Writing in the *Financial Times* on 9 August 2011, Professor Rogoff warned: 'For all intents and purposes, most European and US economies have never fully exited the downturn, with output per capita still below its pre-crisis peak.'

The general malaise has overshadowed all manner of corporate announcements during the 2008–12 period, forcing companies and their PR advisers to explain their strategies in the context of a European downturn and weak economic confidence. Questions over how companies are dealing with the euro-zone crisis have become a major feature in PR planning – even though most clients are reluctant to be drawn into verdicts about EU debt-management – until the financial problems are finally resolved.

'The most direct remedy, of course, would be to find expeditious approaches to cleaning up balance sheets whilst maintaining the integrity of the financial system,' according to Professor Rogoff. He continues:

In the case of Europe, this involves very large debt write-downs in the smaller periphery countries, combined with a German guarantee of central government debt in the rest. In return, Germany will have to receive a disproportionate share of fiscal power in a more deeply integrated union, for at least as long as it is making substantial transfers. In the case of the US, policymakers need to offer schemes to write down underwater mortgages, perhaps in return for other concessions such as giving the lender a share of any future home price appreciation.

Continued disagreements over both diagnosis and cure for the global economy, combined with a series of corporate calamities and self-doubt in the media industry, have made the life of corporate messengers much less predictable. Whether representing debt-laden governments or troubled companies, the downturn has made it harder to protect reputations at the end of the current quadrennial than it was at the beginning.

During the cycle, the business media has become generally more aggressive in its corporate coverage, perhaps reflecting its determination to remain relevant and influential in the face of its own reputational challenge. A media industry struggling to come to terms with a digital business model, fewer resources and a crisis – in the UK – over editorial standards, is clearly more difficult to do business with. Newspapers have cut staff and held down pay in a bid to reset their business models. Hundreds of US newspapers have closed, confronted by the digital revolution. In this quadrennial, online advertising revenues surpassed print ads for the first time. 'Financially the tipping point also has come,' says the Pew Research Center in the USA in *State of the News Media 2011: An Annual Report on American Journalism.* 'The problem for news is that by far the largest share of that online ad revenue goes to non-news sources, particularly to aggregators.'

The growing power of online platforms from Google to Baidu, Facebook or Twitter has only served to increase the anxiety among traditional media outlets – in which public trust has been eroding. Even the Guardian Media Group (GMG), the UK's champion of all things digital, has warned of significant job cutbacks and that it will run out of money in three to five years if no action is taken. As reported in the *FT* on 24 June 2011, GMG chief executive Andrew Miller said, when unveiling a £25 million cost-cutting programme: 'I wanted to leave everybody under no illusion of exactly where we are. Change is with us for many, many years to come.'

Some media organisations anticipated the scale of the upheaval at the start of the current quadrennial. Glen Moreno, chairman of Pearson, the education publisher and owner of the *Financial Times*, says that the company took a hundred of its senior managers to Silicon Valley five years ago to assess the impact of new technology and to formulate a response strategy. 'Digital initiatives are transforming our business model,' Moreno told the Enders Analysis annual conference in 2012. 'Roughly 30% of our revenues now come from business areas that we were not in five years ago. Our challenge is how do we strategically manage down our legacy businesses to prevent previously valuable analogue assets from becoming liabilities.'

The analogue–digital transition in newspapers, which are locked in a race against time to build new subscription revenues faster than the rate of advertising decline, has intensified rapidly over the past four years. The disruptive impact of new technologies has similarly transformed the way large companies and their PR advisers interact with external audiences.

In 2008, few companies or their advisers used social media platforms to respond to reputation threats, or to rebut speculative news articles. By 2012 companies were routinely using Twitter and Facebook to defend their reputations, bypassing traditional media to reach an estimated audience of more than 500 million people using web-linked mobile devices.

The potential for new forms of engagement has prompted the launch of hundreds of digital agencies, each promising to manage online campaigns or offering social media tactics. Their engagement tactics have become more and more elaborate, desperate to connect with the web-community. In one vivid example, the organisers of the 2012 Super Bowl launched a social media command centre where teams of digital specialists monitored conversations on various social media channels, enabling them to track sentiment about the US sporting calendar's set piece event. Companies are following suit, engaging directly with audiences that previously might have been reached only by press release.

Rapid changes in new technology have created new tools for the PR industry to protect hard-won reputations. Those tools span the use of digital platforms for everything from management blogs, tweeting corporate announcements to virtual town-hall meetings and darker practices such as electronic manipulation of online commentary.

The laundering allegations, particularly against London-based firms that do not face the same regulations as their US counterparts, are set to continue into the next business cycle as more governments and more international companies try to promote a cleaner image to the English-speaking world. Such efforts are an easy target for the media, which is exercised by most forms of reputation management.

The controversial practice has high-profile advocates, who regard it as an entirely legitimate business model, such as Alastair Campbell, Tony Blair's former director of communications. 'Is it a bad thing that London has become the world capital for reputation management, including for leaders we would not want running our own country?' he asks in the *FT* on 12 March 2011. 'If all that PR companies do is advise undemocratic countries on how to stay undemocratic, it is right to look down on the work they do. If, on the other hand, the advice leads the countries concerned to move down the road to free societies, we should not rush to judgement on London's role and reputation.' Campbell has subsequently announced plans to join London agency Portland.

The PR industry is divided over how to respond to criticism of such activities, and how to navigate the broader challenges of the quadrennial. Some agencies are rushing into digital activism; others are touting for business as reputation managers for dubious regimes. Some are internationalising as rapidly as possible, while others are reorganising into specialist boutiques.

At WPP, Sir Martin Sorrell diagnosed the problem and the potential solution on the eve of the current four-year cycle. Writing in his 2007 annual report, the WPP chief executive said:

> Clients still require, first and foremost, creativity and great creative ideas. Second, but increasingly, they want better co-ordination (although it is no good co-ordinating a lousy idea). Finally, they want it at the lowest possible price. The challenge is therefore to provide the best ideas in the best co-ordinated or integrated way at the lowest price. To respond to this, the super-agencies will in turn need to focus on attracting, retaining and developing the best talent, structuring their organisations in the most effective way and incentivising their people successfully – qualitatively and quantitatively.

Five years later, it is not clear that the public relations industry has risen to that challenge. A number of agencies are reconsidering their models and staffing structures amid volatile fee income and increasing competitor pressures from new rivals.

The upheaval of the past four years shows no sign of slowing down. The scale of digital challenge, a threat of increased regulation and a media environment which no longer plays by the old rules of engagement is forcing the PR industry to reconfigure its services. Agencies are trying to repurpose themselves for a new, less predictable and potentially less profitable future.

Firms are adapting for a permanent climate of reputation anxiety. Many are reconsidering the sort of clients they want to represent, and reassessing the risk-benefits of the full-service model, spanning everything from public affairs to product marketing, against a strategic focus on one particular discipline. Such reviews reflect growing market competition, with new agencies and solo practitioners jostling for clients and fees.

The climate of introspection is not confined to PR alone. Other businesses are struggling with similar challenges. In a lament that would resonate with PR practitioners, one businessman told columnist Thomas L. Friedman:

> We never really competed against freelancers before. Our competition used to be firms of similar size and capability. We used to do similar things in somewhat different ways, and each other was able to find a niche and make a living.
>
> Today the dynamic is totally different. Our competition is not only those firms which we always used to compete against. Now we have to deal with giant firms, who have the capability to handle small, medium, and large jobs, and also with the solo practitioners working out of their home offices, who (by making use of today's technology and software) can theoretically do the same thing that a person sitting in our office can do … The technology and software are so empowering that it makes us all look the same. In the last month we have lost three jobs to freelance solo practitioners who used to work with companies and have experience and then just went out on their own. Our clients all said the same thing to us: 'Your firm was really qualified. John was very qualified. John was cheaper.' We used to feel bad losing to another firm, but now we're losing to another *person*![24]

---

[24] T.L. Friedman, *The World is Flat*, London, Penguin, 2006.

This sort of grief process is being played out at countless PR agencies facing increased competition and changing client demands. At the end of the current quadrennial, numerous firms are redefining themselves. Different PR players in different markets have embarked on various tactics to defend their role as effective advisers. Some claim to be reputation specialists; others seek the mantle of strategic counsel. Another category wants to be defined as communications risk managers. The next four-year business cycle will determine which model succeeds. But no industry standard has been established; and little agreement has been achieved on how to define – let alone market – the new world of 'reputation management'.

PART THREE

Good Reputations;
Bad Reputations

CHAPTER 17

Reputation Management

In the meeting rooms of the Roppongi Hills Mori Tower, home to the offices of Goldman Sachs in Tokyo, there is a warning sign on every table. It reminds officials what to do in the event of an earthquake. Should the 54-storey building begin to sway, bankers are advised to dive under the nearest desk.

Asked whether the warning was a metaphor for the reputation crisis engulfing Goldman Sachs, one senior official grimaced. 'We've got nowhere to hide, so I'm not sure it would do much good,' he remarked.

From Tokyo to New York, and in other major business centres between, companies have watched in alarm as corporate titans such as Goldman Sachs have been chastised. The bank's discomfort has prompted companies across other industries to reassess the PR and reputation management tactics. A few days before Goldman found itself in the spotlight again – when departing equity derivatives trader Greg Smith lambasted his employer in the *New York Times* – the communications leaders of some of the world's largest corporations gathered in Manhattan for a summit on reputation preservation.

In the spring of 2012, global vice-presidents from companies including Alcoa, GE, Procter & Gamble, Pfizer and Verizon – among others – met at the New Yorker Hotel to compare notes on how to mitigate crisis and reputation risks. Gary Sheffer, vice-president of communications and public affairs at GE, told the audience that reputation management

> has really gone from a command and control kind of thing into a discussion with your stakeholders both internally and externally. Social media has certainly changed that, because you don't own your brand exclusively

anymore. It's owned by the folks on the Internet talking about you every day. Every three seconds we see something posted online about GE – if you are not out there engaging in a discussion with people authentically, you're losing out, because they are going to create perceptions about you that you may not like.

How this is going to evolve is unknown to me. If you had asked me five years ago about where we're going to be today, I would never guess where we are. It is 24 hours a day. It is much better if you [engage] on a regular rather than sporadic basis. That means relationship building, out-reach, partnerships, authentic discussions about the issues we face as big companies – if you do that on a regular basis and not just talk to people when there is a known issue, that will be successful. So intuitively that tells me we need more people. We need smart people to talk about big issues such as health care and energy, and to do it in a way that is productive rather than confrontational.[25]

Such proactive reputation management has emerged as one of the growth areas in corporate communications and external public relations. In a PR market characterised by a loss of media control and a general slowdown in previously lucrative areas of business such as mergers and acquisitions, both clients and their agencies are reconfiguring their communications competence under the broad umbrella of reputation.

The so-called reputation economy is crowded with consultants promising all manner of services. There is little agreement on definitions, process or execution. There is no consensus on which in-house department at large companies 'owns' the reputation issue, or which type of external adviser should handle it. In some companies it is seen as the responsibility of the

---

[25] www.ethicalcorp.com

boardroom audit committee, in others it is an issue for the chief risk officer. Corporate communications has a clear stake in the subject, but often finds itself battling for primacy against legal counsel, marketing, brand management and corporate planning. Among external advisers, PR companies, management consultants, law firms, academics and specialist reputation analysts are all seeking a piece of the action.

The range of voices claiming reputation competence is proving a threat as well as an opportunity. Few companies have yet to establish clear rules of engagement or a standard operating procedure for reputation issues. And many PR agencies are struggling to insert themselves in a meaningful way into the reputation debate.

A leading lawyer involved in one of the landmark crises of 2011 warns that confusion over reputation management poses a major risk for companies. 'Corporate anxiety is evident for everyone to see,' she says. 'What is not so evident is what clear steps companies are taking to address it. They are all worrying about reputation without taking action. They will all tell you how important their reputation is, but then often allow the issue to drift.'

The myriad definitions and collective business anxiety about reputation have, nevertheless, created an opportunity for specialist firms to sell new kinds of services. They include the Global Reptrak 100, an annual survey of the world's most reputable companies compiled by America's Reputation Institute, which claims to be a pioneer in the field of brand and reputation management.

Dr Charles Fombrun, chairman of the institute, says: 'The greater the reputation of the company, the more support it earns from consumers, the better its operating performance, and the more money investors are willing to pay for its shares. This is a key feature of the emerging reputation economy we now live in.'[26]

---

[26] www.reputationinstitute.com

In an attempt to calibrate winners and losers of the reputation economy, the institute polls 48,000 consumers in 15 countries each year. The 2011 survey ranked Google as the most reputable global company followed by Apple. The US company behind the iPad and iPhone displaced Sony from the number two spot following turmoil at the Japanese group over hacker attacks on its PlayStation network. Sony fell to sixth place behind the Walt Disney Co., BMW and Lego.

The ranking of 100 companies, however, offers only an aftermarket snapshot of reputation based on consumer opinion. It does not reflect a company's reputation management competence, its crisis policies or the ability to recover from a major disaster. As a result, almost all of the companies in the ranking are, one way or another, consumer facing or household names. There are six airlines in the line-up and eight carmakers, along with a clutch of retailers, IT companies and fast-moving consumer goods businesses. But there are no banks or insurers, and precious few companies from the BRIC economies.

The partial nature of such rankings is a further symptom of the wide disparity in reputation analysis and definition. More than two dozen speciality journals, from *Corporate Reputation Review* to the *British Journal of Management* and *Administrative Science Quarterly*, regularly publish papers on reputation issues and the latest research. More than 1,500 articles were published in the period from 1996 to 2007, according to a review of corporate reputation literature in *Corporate Reputation Review*, 2010, which identified a wide range of definitions and theories – few of which lend themselves to an overarching phraseology for the subject. 'There are two major problems with viewing corporate reputation as an aggregate perception,' says Kent Walker, of the Asper School of Business at the University of Manitoba. Writing in *Corporate Reputation Review*, he adds:

The first problem is that reputation is often issue specific. A corporation may have a particular, and potentially different, reputation for each of the following issues: profitability, environmental responsibility, social responsibility, employee treatment, corporate governance, and product quality. For example, Wal-Mart has an excellent reputation for profitability, but a poor one for employee treatment. The second problem is that the corporation may have a different reputation per stakeholder group … Wal-Mart had a tough reputation with suppliers but a good reputation with customers and investors.

Wal-Mart's reputation for probity was dealt a severe blow in 2012 when the *New York Times* reported that the retailer's largest foreign operation, in Mexico, had allegedly paid bribes and that an internal investigation into the matter had been suppressed at the group's headquarters in Arkansas.

The increasing frequency of such corporate scandals has prompted many large companies to review their risk policies, taking greater account of reputational threats. But few agree on how to define, let alone manage, reputation risk.

The lack of any industry standard has enabled PR agencies and other advisers to adopt their own view of how and why reputation matters. Even where attempts at a single definition have been attempted, they are so vague that any number of advisers can claim some level of expertise in the area. The most commonly used academic definition was set back in 1996 by Dr Fombrun, now chairman of the Reputation Institute. Opening the way for multiple interpretations, he defined overall corporate reputation as: 'A relatively stable, issue specific aggregate perceptual representation of a company's past actions and future prospects compared against some standard.'[27]

But that summary is sufficiently open-ended that it risks multiple interpretations. The potential for confusion has not

---

[27] C.J. Fombrun, *Reputation: Realizing Value from the Corporate Image*, Boston, Harvard Business School Press, 1996.

been helped by academic attempts to apply formulas to reputation. In language that terrifies most PR executives, academics have tried to define reputation based on correlation and regression analysis, along with so-called 'exogenous variables'. In one article for *Corporate Reputation Review*, such analysis was used by three academics to create a model that defined reputation for social and environmental responsibility as ($F(1, 172) = 4.45, p < 0.035$, adjusted $R^2 = 0.02$). The same study defined emotional appeal as ($F(1, 172) = 5.42, p < 0.021$, adjusted $R^2 = 0.03$).

These sorts of statistics create little more than migraines among PR advisers and their clients. While they all want to manage their reputations more effectively, they care mainly about the practical application of strategies and tactics rather than the bone dry theories behind them. But there is one academic finding upon which both advisers and clients probably agree – the theory of 'media system dependency'.

First defined in 1976, the theory sets out how the news media shapes reputations among audiences with limited access to information. Explaining how media system dependency had evolved over the intervening 34 years, academics from universities in the USA, Germany and Switzerland wrote in a 2010 paper in *Corporate Reputation Review* that:

> Firms, as part of the economic system, depend upon the news media to reach their stakeholders and to foster their reputation among those individuals or groups who contribute to its wealth creating capacity and activities. Firms depend upon the news media in particular for the dissemination of such information that cannot be directly experienced through consumption or interaction and that lacks credibility when communicated by the firms themselves ... The news media, on the other hand, depend on firms for content that is of interest to their audiences, and oftentimes they rely on firms to make revenues from advertising.

This is the marketplace in which the PR industry seeks to flourish.

Companies still rely on PR advisers as intermediaries to promote or defend their reputation to the media. The media in turn treats PR companies as an information resource, from which to collate content and context to inform their readers. That, at least, is how the interrelationship between corporations, their advisers and the media tended to work in the latter half of the twentieth century.

PR firms would traditionally determine which media needed most intensive management when it came to protecting a client's reputation, or which media to feed with information that might promote external perceptions. Clients, meanwhile, would expect their agencies to have a firm grasp on which media outlets had the greatest influence on stakeholder decision-making, particularly in the investor and analyst community. Working together, a company and its advisers would thus execute their reputation management plan.

A PR campaign prepared by one of the USA's largest companies, facing a crisis in recent years, demonstrates this linear approach to reputation management. Entitled 'Communicating into a Headwind ... Changing Minds, Changing Perceptions', the strategy document details the assumptions, action elements, objectives, strategy and messages to be deployed in rebuilding the company's reputation.

Among the assumptions, the company admitted that 'media coverage will continue at an extremely high level and mostly negative tone for several more months', and warned: 'as we knock down each negative we will be presented with a new one for some time to come'. Together with its agency advisers, the company embarked on a wide-ranging internal, national and market specific campaign to plant 'game-changing stories and engage key influentials'. It also included a social media programme of blogs, podcasts, enthusiasts' networks, customer communities and new video applications in an attempt to protect the company's reputation.

The scope of the campaign reflected the changing nature of PR and broader reputation management from a linear relationship with print media to a wider exercise in managing expectations among multiple digitally-connected audiences. Of those audiences, two factors are making media behaviour harder to predict: widespread journalistic scepticism towards corporate conduct generally, and a breakdown in traditional rules of media engagement.

That breakdown was predicted back in 2008 as the financial crisis mounted. 'We are about to enter a fractured, chaotic world of news, characterised by superior community conversation but a decidedly diminished level of first rate journalism,' according to US media critic Eric Alterman. Writing in the *New Yorker* on 31 March 2008, he added: 'The transformation of newspapers from enterprises devoted to objective reporting to a cluster of communities, each engaged in its own kind of "news" – and each with its own set of "truths" upon which to base debate and discussion – will mean the loss of a single national narrative and agreed-upon set of "facts" by which to conduct our politics.'

Fissures in the old command and control system of media engagement have served to heighten corporate anxiety about the precarious nature of business reputation.

Companies rightly regard their reputation as one of their most important intangible assets. But the traditional pipeline to market – the media – can no longer be relied upon to distinguish between fact and fiction. At the same time, a converging number of advisers, academics and management specialists are trying to sell reputation services to increasingly confused purchasers.

In trying to carve out a role and income stream from the new reputation environment, PR agencies are restating their relevance for this uncertain marketplace. Some firms argue that it is not possible to manage reputations across the entire digital landscape; so it is better to focus on relationships of trust and media that carries real influence. It also requires an injection of reputation management into early-stage corporate decision-making, rather than managing the fallout once a commercial strategy has been implemented.

No amount of reputation management can save a company that is failing to perform or failing to deliver a coherent strategy. A good reputation needs 'proof points' that demonstrate a company deserves the reputation it aspires to. In other words, today's media environment demands public relations without spin. 'People are interested in the facts, but not the tendentious, selective presentation of them,' says the leader of one international agency. 'This also affects how companies and their officers communicate – there is a greater premium attached to telling it like it is, and not overselling, embellishing, deceiving.'

This direct, plain facts approach reflects one way to navigate the confusion over rules and definitions in reputation management. Not all audiences are willing to give companies the benefit of the doubt. Given that distrust, many agencies are, therefore, advising clients to focus on issues that they can still control and media outlets that they can still trust. By doing so, they are joining the growing number of advisers applying risk management tools to their services. How a company articulates and conveys its reputation is a matter of risk, where you hope that clarity and trust will secure a favourable outcome.

The issue of trust goes to the heart of reputation management. If it is impossible to trust how information will be treated by external audiences then PR agencies will focus increasingly on counterparties – particularly in the media – that they can trust to give them a fair hearing. That sentiment is shared by elements of the media, which want to be trusted recipients of corporate information. In their own crowded market, media outlets believe it is a competitive advantage to remain an outlet of record. 'I used to think, as I think a lot of people did, that the proliferation of alternative outlets of information and journalism was somehow a mortal peril to us,' said Marcus Brauchli, executive editor of the *Washington Post*, in the 3rd Richard S. Salant

Lecture on freedom of the press, given at Harvard University on 28 October 2010:

> My thinking has evolved, and I now think this ever-deepening ocean of information actually favors islands of clarity. If you are an organization that practices good journalism and is providing people with good and reliable information, they will seek you out.
>
> In a sense you look for those places you can trust and you can rely upon, rather than depend on sources of information that are flawed. Maybe that is wishful thinking, but the evidence suggests that it is working, that the places that do produce good journalism in fact do drive the biggest audiences.

PR agencies that have a supply-side relationship with outlets such as the *Washington Post* should also seek to provide islands of clarity, built on good and reliable information.

Amid all the confusion about reputation management, it is now up to senior PR advisers to deliver context without spin to a growing number of audiences. The range and complexity of those audiences does not lend itself to easy management. They require careful handling and a targeted approach that balances opportunity against risk. That balancing act is hard enough in periods of corporate calm. In a crisis, it is extremely difficult to get right. As a business challenge, this equation is emerging as the new defining trend in the PR industry: can your advisers manage risk?

CHAPTER 18

Risky Business

In the chairman's office at Anglo-American, Sir John Parker keeps mementos of a career at the riskier end of British heavy industry. There are maritime pictures – a reminder of his period at Harland and Wolff, the Belfast shipyard where he was chairman and chief executive during some of the darkest times of Northern Ireland's troubles. On the sideboard, there is a framed photograph of Sir John down a mine. It was taken shortly after he joined the board of British Coal in the mid-1980s, as the company struggled to rebuild its reputation following one of the ugliest industrial disputes of the twentieth century.

As non-executive chairman of one of the world's largest mining companies, the softly spoken Ulsterman has an acute sense of global risk and the sort of threats faced by companies exposed to safety, environmental and regulatory scrutiny. 'Management everywhere has to reassess what risks they can control,' says Sir John, who is a visiting fellow at Oxford University's Centre for Corporate Reputation. 'Where we see risks that are difficult to manage, it is vital to know if it is a high probability event and whether it will spin out of control if it hits us.'

Sir John is one of a growing band of industrialists to highlight the linkage between operational risks and corporate reputation. He sees it as a core priority for the boards of Anglo-American and other businesses, particularly following the spate of damaging headlines about crisis-hit companies in recent years.

His concerns are echoed by other non-executive directors and business advisers. 'Managing reputation risk in today's business environment cannot be considered a second or third order priority,' says David Stulb, the global leader of Fraud Investigation & Dispute Services at Ernst & Young in the company's business risk report for 2009. 'Effective reputation risk management must start with the Board ... Boards should consider making the reputation risk an agenda item at all meetings, and should give thought to mandating the explicit assessment of reputational risks in all business decisions they take.'

The appointment of chief risk officers, boardroom risk committees and the adoption by many companies of 'strategic risk frameworks' have opened a new front in the advisory battlefield, with all sorts of rival consultancies claiming risk management credentials. Just as reputation – in all its guises – is redefining the world of corporate communications, so risk-measurement is emerging as another new buzzword for PR firms hoping to differentiate their services.

Risk management skills have become more important for PR agencies in the wake of communication failures at several large companies, where in most cases the initial crisis response made matters worse rather than better. The calamities at companies including Nokia, Olympus and Wal-Mart – although all different in cause-and-effect – have forced corporate boards and their shareholders to demand better risk advice.

One leading international fund manager, with £170 billion of assets under management, has expressed major reservations about the quality and depth of risk assessment: 'There are far too many crises arising for us, on behalf of shareholders, to be comfortable that companies are looking at risks comprehensively and developing strategies to mitigate them. Our concern as shareholders is that if these risks aren't contained reputational damage will arise that ultimately harms our returns.'

Such warnings have prompted reviews across industry about whether risk management policies reflect the growing threats to corporate reputation. In turn, PR companies and other advisers are rushing to adopt best practice in risk-profiling. Their move into this increasingly lucrative but challenging segment follows warnings that many companies are ill-prepared for this scale and pace of reputational threats.

Groups including AIG, the US financial services giant, as well as Enron, Arthur Andersen, BP, Northern Rock, Railtrack, Firestone and Airbus have all been cited as classic case studies of how not to manage risks. In most of them, the boards were ineffective in terms of failing to monitor or address risks. Enron's board was selected mainly from friends of the chairman or beneficiaries of Enron's political and charitable donations. Likewise, AIG's board mainly comprised friends and colleagues of Hank Greenberg, the chief executive forced to resign following allegations of fraudulent accounting. And the board of BP was criticised following the Texas City refinery explosion for the gap between its high ideals and the day-to-day practise of the company's operations.

In a report commissioned by Airmic, the risk management association, researchers found that many of these companies failed to recognise and manage risks in seven key areas which were beyond the reach of traditional risk analysis and management techniques.

'Several of the firms we studied were destroyed by the crises that struck them. While others survived, they often did so with their reputations in tatters and faced an uphill task in rebuilding their businesses,' said the Airmic report, *Roads to Ruin*, 2011, compiled by Cass Business School. 'We found that the firms most badly affected had underlying weaknesses that made them especially prone both to crises and to the escalation of the crisis into a disaster.'

Of the seven weaknesses identified by the report, defective communication was named as a major threat alongside boardroom incompetence, directors' 'blindness' to reputation issues, poor leadership culture, excessive complexity, inappropriate incentives and a general lack of importance applied to risk management and internal audit work. Researchers at Cass Business School also noted a causal link between weaknesses in leaders and board composition with respect to so-called soft skills – staffing, style and values – and the propensity to suffer major reputational crises.

After studying more than 20 corporations with pre-crisis assets of more than $6,000 billion, the researchers concluded that many companies had failed to address underlying risks to their business areas. Internal communication, or the lack of it, has been identified as one of the most serious risks preventing information from flowing freely around an organisation. In examples familiar to the PR community, the Cass report also warned that poor communication internally undermined efforts to safeguard external reputation.

At BP, years before the Deepwater Horizon accident, weak communication was identified as a worrying problem following the Texas City refinery fire. 'Poor vertical communication meant that there was no adequate early warning of problems and no means of understanding the growing problems on the site,' investigators noted. 'BP's approach to decentralisation also meant that top management had not effectively communicated its priorities, including those on safety, to its operating units.'

Had a thorough reputation risk test been applied to BP following Texas City, it might have identified three problem areas that PR initiatives could have addressed. Firstly, it would have demonstrated the dysfunction and tension between the corporate communications department in London and the public affairs office in Washington DC. Secondly, it would have alerted the management and board of BP to a wide perception gap between how the company thought it was seen in the USA and the reality of public opinion, which regarded the oil and energy group as still on probation following highly publicised safety lapses.

Lastly, and most importantly given subsequent events around Deepwater Horizon, such a test would have shown that BP was engaging with the wrong government departments in safeguarding its US reputation. In the run-up to the Gulf of Mexico spill, the company's lobbying efforts were focused mainly on the Energy Department and Environment Protection Agency. Had BP engaged in intensive negotiations with the National Security

Agency, it might have established a degree of 'reputation credit' as one of the energy exploration companies helping to guarantee future oil independence for the USA. When it comes to energy, securing future supplies is a national security issue for the US administration. If BP had been seen as a company contributing positively to such security it might have moderated the White House reaction when Deepwater Horizon occurred. Such reputation engagement would not have averted the crisis, but it might have dissuaded American politicians, the media and community groups from going to war against the company with such devastating effects for its global standing.

Failure to project reputational strengths before a crisis was one of many problems highlighted by academics studying corporate shortcomings. If a company has not built up a healthy balance of reputation credit before a crisis, the scale of the deficit it suffers when a problem occurs is always much worse.

Such danger signals are compounded when risk managers or outside advisers do not have sufficient influence or a direct line to the board to raise their concerns. The Cass report cited Société Générale, the French bank, as a classic example of a failure to pass bad news upwards through an organisation. In 2008, as the financial crisis was sweeping global markets, the bank found that Jerome Kerviel, one of its traders, had lost almost €5 billion. Subsequent investigations revealed that internal queries had been raised several months earlier but were not followed up. 'More than 70 oddities associated with his trading were reported internally, but the compliance officer was unable to challenge Kerviel or get the attention of his superiors. Clearly, companies are exposed to unnecessary risk when the status of their risk and compliance teams is so low that they cannot do their job effectively,' concluded the researchers.

In a wake-up call for the industry, the report called for a sweeping rethink of the scope, purpose and practicalities of risk management as well as better skills training, enhanced role and status for risk professionals, and a system to ensure that so-called missing risks are identified earlier.

These recommendations pose a challenge to PR firms because their work traditionally covers reputation repair rather than crisis avoidance. To win potential fees in the burgeoning risk management sector, PR practitioners will need to demonstrate that they can anticipate, measure, prioritise and understand complex areas of corporate risk. The changeover will not be easy, particularly for legacy PR firms whose business model rests primarily on post-crisis damage limitation and media engagement. Given that risk assessment is outside the core competence of most PR firms, agencies also need to be able to convince clients that they are better placed than other consultants to advise on such issues. Certainly, few PR executives would claim to be experts in what McKinsey calls the 'risk triggers' of inflation, technology, public policy regulation, commodity prices, pandemics, demographics and geopolitical events – among many others.

The industry's challenge is to identify areas where proven PR expertise is vital in minimising risk and promoting reputation. It will be hard for public relations to capture business in areas such as predictive analytics given existing expertise from rival service providers around succession planning, supply chain interruptions and customer relationship management. But there is a significant business opportunity in helping boards and executives to navigate and better prepare for how the media can be managed in a crisis.

Given the continued dependency of most large corporations on media coverage to influence its stakeholders, PR expertise should become part of the risk management planning process – particularly in a digital era. The potential business opportunity was identified in 2011 by Deloitte, the accounting and consultancy firm, in a report – *The Risk Intelligent CFO: Converting Risk into Opportunity* – which highlighted areas where public relations could augment risk management.

'The ability of social media to instantly broadcast corporate missteps dramatically shortens the amount of time a company has to manage a blunder,' said Deloitte.

> With more online retailers encouraging customers to rate their purchases, too many critical reviews can discourage shoppers from buying the company's product. Blog entries and tweets, whether accurate or not, can make potentially damaging information immediately available to customers, shareholders, and the media. Even more daunting is the fact that some online entities exist for the sole purpose of shining a spotlight on secret corporate information.

The firm urged companies to create 'capital stress tests' that cover key areas of reputational risk, major areas of compliance, and the effectiveness and maturity of the compliance and risk management process. A number of PR companies have developed models for such stress tests, hoping to harness risk expertise that they can charge for and which could help convert crisis projects into long-term retained mandates around risk avoidance.

Winning a risk management mandate would be a vote of confidence in the PR industry's ability to diversify its service proposition. But delivering meaningful results from a stress test or reputation audit will be the real determinant of whether communication firms can succeed in this area. Most so-called perception studies, undertaken by PR firms, are a costly exercise in telling a client about opinions they already know or which they suspect exist. Agencies should improve their analysis of such research and come up with strategic recommendations to defend a client's reputation against potential risks that have been identified for the first time.

So far, the PR industry's attempts to cash in on the risk sector have delivered mixed results. Many companies are not convinced that the media advisers are best placed to assess a complex range of vulnerabilities. That view is echoed by some of the specialist firms quantifying reputation risk.

Basil Towers, who leads Hesleden, a leading organisational research practice specialising in corporate reputation, found that PR agencies barely figure in the current risk management considerations of many large companies. After interviewing executives from more than 200 companies between 2008 and 2012, Towers calculated that less than 5 per cent of those questioned saw a role for PR firms as strategic risk advisers.

'Agencies don't know how to adapt,' says Towers. 'PR firms are finding it difficult to adjust to an environment where corporate affairs officers are having a much greater responsibility for risk; a world where reputation is being factored into performance management and measurement; and where institutional shareholders are beginning to fit reputation into analytical models.'

If PR firms are to move into risk management, it seems clear that they must develop some sort of compelling competitive advantage over other advisers. One route into the risk arena might be to exploit PR expertise as intermediaries not just between a company and the media, but within a company between executive functions and the board. This could help improve co-ordination on reputation issues, which is frequently cited as a major corporate weakness.

The potential role of PR adviser as reputational intermediary was first mooted in a major report on reputation and its risks by two agencies based in the USA and Switzerland. Robert G. Eccles and Scott C. Newquist, founders of Perception Partners, a Florida-based corporate governance and risk analysis firm, teamed up with Roland Schatz, chief executive of the Media Tenor Institute for Media Analysis in Lugano, to identify how companies should manage risks before a problem or crisis strikes.

They blamed poor co-ordination in decision-making by different business units and functions for creating major reputation risks. In the February 2007 issue of *Harvard Business Review*, the risk specialists wrote:

> Investor relations (with varying degrees of input from the CFO and CEO) attempts to ascertain and influence the expectations of analysts and investors; marketing surveys customers, advertising buys ads that shape expectations; HR surveys employees; corporate communications monitors the media and conveys the company's messages; corporate social responsibility engages with NGOs; and corporate affairs monitors new and pending laws and regulations. All of these actions are important to understanding and managing reputational risks. But more often than not, these groups do a bad job of sharing information or co-ordinating their plans.

They urged agencies to replace old tools such as clipping services with strategic media intelligence, which places the coverage of a company in a broader industry context. Other recommendations included calling for a closer liaison with in-house crisis management teams or with a company's chief risk officer – where they exist.

The awareness of reputational risk across industry has continued to grow over the course of the 2008–12 quadrennial, the four-year period which began with the global financial crisis, was punctuated by major corporate disasters and drew to a close with the removal of several high profile chief executives from crisis-hit companies. Defending such companies has been a reputational challenge in itself for the PR industry – a task that it has sometimes struggled to excel at.

Agencies now have an opportunity to exploit the business world's increased appetite for reputation risk management. They may succeed in this emerging business area only if they can establish a credible niche, connecting their media expertise and communication skills to proven risk analysis.

Sitting in the chairman's office at Anglo-American, Sir John Parker predicts strong demand for advisory services that can mitigate reputational dangers. 'The ability of outside advisers to show us the lessons that must be learned and how to upgrade our response capability for a catastrophic event is extremely important,' he says. 'And if these advisers can help us deal with such problems locally and nationally, or further mitigate the potential of these events happening, then that would be extremely valuable.'

CHAPTER 19

Constant Vigilance

The Serious Fraud Office (SFO) did not knock. The UK country manager of a leading global corporation came home to find his front door off its hinges. Police officers and agents from the fraud squad were boxing up documents, opening cabinets and preparing to remove computers.

Raids were also underway at the homes and offices of other executives, sending shockwaves through the company and alarming its suppliers and customers. The media relished the scenes, publishing breathless stories that compounded the sense of crisis among managers of the accused business.

At the group's headquarters, a crisis committee was rapidly convened to co-ordinate the response strategy. The chief executive was determined to challenge the legal basis and conduct of the raids, robustly rejecting suggestions of corrupt procurement practices. Other members of the committee drew up plans to defend the company's ongoing reputation.

'We are not a dirty business, so we had to show that we were the victims of wrongful arrests and unacceptable action by a fraud agency trying to justify its own future,' recalls one of the executives involved. 'It was essential to reassure customers that we observed all the rules in securing contracts and delivering first-class products. We were extremely vigilant about our business practices.'

The crisis committee – comprising top management, legal counsel, the chief ethics officer and communications specialists – felt partially vindicated when a British High Court judge subsequently chastised the SFO for sheer incompetence over separate raids involving property tycoon Vincent Tchenguiz. As reported in the *Financial Times* on 4 April 2012, Lord Justice Thomas, president of the Queen's Bench division and one of the most senior judicial figures in England, told the fraud agency that the details of how it put together its case were 'profoundly unsatisfactory'.

Criticism of the smash and grab tactics by the SFO might represent a PR victory for those accused. The agency's own reputation is now on the line. But that is modest compensation for the reputational damage already inflicted on individuals such as Mr Tchenguiz, who was targeted in dawn raids involving more than 130 officers more than a year before the High Court's withering verdict.

News of such raids is red meat for a hungry media pack. Allegations of corporate wrongdoing always rank higher up the news list than business success stories. Anxious to avoid being the next front page story, a number of leading companies have now moved on to a permanent crisis footing. But it has taken a series of major crises to persuade them to act.

'One of the things that most companies are not good at is having their crisis team ready in advance,' says a leading London-based lawyer specialising in reputation repair work. 'The lesson of the latest crisis cycle has been that companies should have a de facto crisis response team ready at all times, composed of a senior independent director – not the chief executive – the in-house communications director, the head of legal, the person leading commercial strategy and a trusted outside PR expert.'

Too often companies convene a crisis committee only after a problem has emerged, and then it tends to be an unwieldy group of competing opinions. One official involved in News International's attempts to contain the phone-hacking crisis said that response meetings sometimes involve more than 30 people, each proposing different approaches to the problem. 'The crisis had already moved on to stage two before we had agreed our response to the first wave of threats,' according to the official. 'The communications response was diabolical because management was in denial. They didn't want to hear bad news; they were not ready to consider ultra-aggressive proposals on how to deal with the problem.'

This inertia is not peculiar to News International. In the corridors of power at numerous companies facing crisis, the sense of disbelief, anger and depression (see Chapter 9) frequently hampers decision-making and delays effective communications strategies. For advisers to companies in crisis, the challenge is to instil a sense of urgency in clients reluctant to believe that their reputations are on the line. It is even harder when senior management and the boards of such companies don't want to listen. Historically, the leaders of most companies have not looked to outside advisers, and particularly not to their PR firms, for preventative measures or crisis avoidance systems. Rather, they have treated them as fixers, a resource to manage the media and limit any broader fallout once a crisis has occurred.

Yet the spectacle of leading brands suffering the consequences of poor crisis management has prompted a slow, inexorable change in corporate tactics. The need for change has intensified with the 'concertina effect' of digital scrutiny, in which social media networks, bloggers and the 'twitterati' can mobilise damaging campaigns against perceived business misconduct.

The sense of unease among business leaders has created a new market opportunity for advisers, including PR firms, to recast themselves as crisis specialists who should be paid for their avoidance skills. But seizing that opportunity is easier said than done. The instinct of most business leaders in a crisis, particularly after its first phase, is to hunker down and hope things will return to normal. These companies are not yet ready to embrace the concept of a permanent crisis committee involving their PR fixers. Even after the high-profile corporate crises of the 2008–12 cycle, it remains the exception rather than the rule for companies to embrace so-called 'adaptive leadership': the willingness to completely reorganise their reputation management strategies.

The scale of the problem was identified several years ago by Cambridge Leadership Associates (CLA), the US advisory firm set up by former tutors at Harvard University's John F. Kennedy School of Government. 'The task of leading during a sustained crisis – whether you are the CEO of a major corporation or a manager heading up an impromptu company initiative – is treacherous,' say Ronald Heifetz and his partners at CLA, writing in the *Harvard Business Review* in 2009. 'Crisis leadership has two distinct phases. First is that emergency phase, when your task is to stabilize the situation and buy time. Second is the adaptive phase, when you tackle the underlying cause of the crisis and build the capacity to thrive in a new reality.'

The test of leadership, they argue, is whether a company and its advisers stick to the old way of doing business or whether they press 'the reset' button to prepare more effectively for any future threat. The danger for companies unwilling to embrace fundamental change is that they will try to solve any crisis with short-term fixes such as cost-cutting and redundancies. 'They'll default to what they know how to do in order to reduce frustration and quell their own and others' fears,' adds Heifetz.

> Their primary mode will be drawing on familiar expertise to help their organizations weather the storm … People who practice what we call *adaptive leadership* do not make this mistake. Instead of hunkering down, they seize the opportunity of moments like the current one to hit the organization's reset button. They use the turbulence of the present to build on and bring closure to the past. In the process, they change the rules of the game, reshape parts of the organization, and redefine the work people do.

Usually in the corporate world, it takes a series of crises for a company to change its behaviour.

Nissan, Japan's second-largest carmaker, has embraced a series of leadership changes and new tactics after suffering both self-inflicted and external crises. The company suffered a near-death experience at the end of the 1990s when internal structural problems over cost control, unprofitable products and an enormous debt load pushed it to the brink of bankruptcy. After almost a decade of restructuring, it was then hit by the financial crisis of 2008 which froze credit markets and undermined consumer demand for high ticket items such as automobiles. Demand fell by 35 per cent in the USA, 20 per cent in Europe and 15 per cent in Japan. Having barely recovered from that downturn, Nissan and other Japanese carmakers were then hit by the earthquake and tsunami of March 2011, which left more than 20,000 people dead and devastated the coastal communities of north-east Japan.

Giving an address entitled 'The New Normal' to the Japan Society on 17 November 2011, Carlos Ghosn, Nissan chief executive, said: 'These were all extremely high-profile crises that threatened to cripple our operations. But in each case, Nissan emerged stronger than before.'

He argued that effective crisis response, of which communications is a core part, requires four basic approaches: firstly, to assess the situation in a lucid and objective manner; secondly, to construct a clear vision with a few key priorities; thirdly, to ensure the entire workforce is motivated to address the problem; and, lastly, to demonstrate that top management is engaged, accountable for achieving results and prepared for the future.

Describing the initial diagnosis phase of a crisis, Ghosn explained:

in 1999, we took three months to listen and understand the situation of Nissan from every perspective – talking to employees, suppliers, dealers, plant union leaders – so that we could form a clear diagnosis of all the issues and build the Nissan Revival Plan.

During the earthquake, the key was quick assessment and rapid response. Literally while the building was still shaking, we created a global disaster control team to ensure employee safety and continuously monitor damage.

The Nissan chief executive, who holds the same role at Renault of France, maintains that effective diagnosis of a crisis has to be followed up by transparent execution of the response strategy, coupled to effective communications with all stakeholders. By doing so, he suggests Nissan has emerged with greater confidence and momentum. 'It will make us even more prepared for the next round of challenges.'

Other companies are embracing similar sorts of crisis preparation and risk management. Although less exposed to the sort of seismic shocks that hit Nissan, Pearson is one of the latest groups to reconsider its approach.

The educational publisher, which also owns Penguin and the *Financial Times*, has overhauled its risk functions to address potential threats against the business. A group of senior executives, including senior members of the communications team, meets regularly to examine various threats to the company's reputation. 'We look at the top 10 risks by likelihood and by potential financial impact,' says one member of the risk assessment team. 'Half of the risks may be purely reputational such as screw ups in exam processing, data losses or criticism of the *FT*'s journalism; the other half are purely financial such as the impact of foreign exchange rates on our business.'

Like several other enlightened companies, both Nissan and Pearson are looking at processes to deal with risks and systematic tools on how to monitor potential threats. Their appetite for more sophisticated measurement systems has fuelled a new market in analytical services, which claims to measure and assess the reputational drivers of value.

Steel City Re, which professes to be a pioneer in the field of quantitative reputation risk services, is typical of the new genre of advisory firms seeking to exploit the era of corporate anxiety. The advisory firm, established in Pittsburgh on the eve of the financial crisis, in 2007, has calculated that diminished reputation can reduce a corporation's value by an average of 7 per cent.

Pointing to the market opportunity for such advisers, Steel City Re cites growing awareness of reputation issues among America's largest companies. In 2011, more than 280 of the S&P 500 constituent members disclosed in their annual filings that reputation risk was material to their enterprise value, compared with just 40 companies that mentioned the issue in their filings of 2008.[28] Steel City Re concludes: 'In an acute reputational crisis, an entity's preexisting reputation can spell the difference between its survival or failure.'

Given that threat, PR agencies and specialist monitoring firms hope that corporations will pay more for reputation analysis. Hence firms such as Investor Dynamics in Britain, one of the new generation of online tracking businesses, promises to apply 'measurement and research to the craft of communications' with 'situational analysis and benchmarking against peers'.

The sheer range of risks measured by such companies is contributing to the widely held sense of unease among leading corporations about different rates of exposure. The risk landscape now stretches all the way from issues such as natural disasters to industrial disputes or from product recalls to cybercrime.

Of those risks, IT hacking by both state-sponsored agencies and malicious IT experts now ranks among the highest business anxieties. According to the *Financial Times*, a report by the UK Cabinet office in 2011 estimated that cyber espionage was costing the UK economy some £17 billion a year. 'German counterintelligence experts have maintained the German economy is losing about €53 billion or the equivalent of 30,000 jobs to economic espionage yearly,' the newspaper reported on 2 June 2011.

---

[28] www.steelcityre.com

The alarming nature of these figures poses a challenge for the PR industry. On the one hand, agencies hope to offer effective therapy for clients seeking reassurance about their risk exposure to such problems. Additionally, agencies would like to be utilised earlier in crisis planning. But on the other hand, traditional PR firms are finding it hard to assert their expertise and relevance in handling complex technical issues, particularly when numerous specialist agencies are emerging to challenge their client relationships.

For PR executives who have grown up regarding themselves as intermediaries between business and the media, it is a difficult leap to become risk management specialists in areas such as commodity prices, foreign exchange, IT cybercrime, regulation and consumer demand. Of course, all self-respecting agencies would claim, in today's environment, a level of competence in risk management systems. But few have made the full transition from post-crisis reputation surgery to 'pre-med' skills in spotting a client's vulnerabilities.

PR specialists equipped with diagnostic insights are not necessarily better placed to win new business. They have to be extremely careful how they tell their clients what's wrong with them and what it will take to get better. Unlike normal clinician–patient relationships, businesses do not always appreciate their weaknesses being identified – albeit confidentially – by outsiders. And significant conflicts often exist within the client organisation, between different executives or between management and the board, over the sort of care plan that will minimise a potential crisis.

Even where clients are ready to acknowledge the need for better crisis preparation, the business case and return on investment for PR advisers is far from clear. When a crisis is in full swing, clients will pay almost any price, bear any burden, to be clear of the problem. But it is harder to charge significant fees for prevention and avoidance tactics. Where mandates exist, clients are tending to gravitate towards project relationships for risk and crisis management, rather than the long-term retained contracts that are vital for PR industry cash flow.

A modest number of clients are adopting new crisis management tactics – at least among those whose instinct is not to hunker down. For these risk-aware companies, there is willingness to include PR advisers in developing early warning indicators and scenario plans. All of that is good news for firms hoping to secure new sources of revenue. The bad news is that many other clients remain to be convinced about the degree of expertise that PR executives bring to the boardroom table, in the area of risk analysis and prevention.

When the chairmen or chief executives of large companies look down the boardroom table, and see their PR advisers vying for attention among other experts, they still tend to regard the PR function as something that will get them out of trouble. Generally, these business leaders are ready to take the PR medicine when they know they are weak. But in a business era where crisis prevention should be preferable to cure, PR advisers have still not secured automatic membership of the preparation team. Some boards are ready to take that gamble. They recognise that reaction times have shrunk, and that reputations have never been more vulnerable. Others have yet to be convinced. They prevaricate before calling in the image-makers; sometimes only when the crisis is underway – or after the Serious Fraud Office has knocked down the door. By then, it is often too late to get your story straight.

CHAPTER 20

Securing a Narrative

A generation ago, a maintenance man at Kungens Kurva, the world's first IKEA store, left his ladders and trellis table in the display area during his lunch break. When he returned, they were gone. A customer had taken them to the check-out, determined to instal the utilitarian furniture in his nearby Stockholm apartment.

IKEA's managers quickly saw the business opportunity. Furniture designed for the tool shed could be marketed for sitting rooms. Cheap chic has been part of IKEA's corporate narrative ever since. Ingvar Kamprad, founder of the Swedish furniture retailer, described the narrative as a 'social ambition': to offer well-designed and functional furniture at prices so low that most people can afford it. Rejecting the idea of a stock market flotation or capital restructuring of the family-owned group, he later insisted that preserving the company's values was more important than diverting profits to dividends or satisfying demands from institutional investors for predictable return on capital. 'Pressure to show constant profit growth would hurt my business idea, which remains to provide affordable furniture for people around the world,' according to Kamprad in the *FT* on 18 August 1998. 'That means making very risky investments in places where we will not make a profit for five years.'

IKEA is today one of many global corporations passionate about its narrative. Controversies over the secretive nature of IKEA's holding structure, tax policies, treatment of suppliers and environmental sustainability have, in recent years, threatened to overshadow the company's carefully constructed image. So the business, whose name derives from its founder's initials, has worked hard to restate its basic purpose. It has also tried to address concerns about its impact on low-cost suppliers and raw materials by becoming the largest corporate donor to UNICEF, and by launching the IKEA 'social initiative' to stress its pro-environment credentials.

Similar campaigns have been launched by companies in multiple industrial sectors, each hoping to polish their reputations as good corporate citizens. Hence, PepsiCo has launched 'Performance with Purpose', and has attempted to build a brand credit for sustainability initiatives in areas such as renewable energy, water use and packaging design. Similarly, GE has long emphasised 'Ecomagination'. ABB promises 'Power and Productivity for a Better World'. Intel claims to be 'Sponsors of Tomorrow', Cisco says it is 'Built for the Human Network' and Sony stands by the tagline 'Make-Believe'.

Such vague and grandiose promises mark the latest convergence of marketing and public relations. In a crowded, hostile, corporate environment companies are anxiously restating what they stand for, hoping to differentiate themselves from competitors and to promote their brand appeal. So business leaders regard a compelling narrative as a tool to explain their vision, the need to become more efficient and to instil a sense of urgency among employees.

Nowhere is the need for a compelling narrative more important, arguably, than at Sony. Sir Howard Stringer, chairman of the Board at the Japanese consumer electronics and media entertainment group, tried to instil a new sense of urgency during his 2005–12 tenure as chief executive. Speaking in 2010, he said: 'The management team at Sony gets it. The younger generation of managers knows that if we're going to be competitive we have to change … When we lost money for the first time, people here saw the scale of the threat. Then our management stopped looking backward, particularly the younger generation of executives. A competitive instinct to survive kicked in.'

After Sir Howard handed over the reins to new chief executive Kazuo Hirai in 2012, Sony vowed to build a new corporate narrative based around interconnected devices handling Sony content across the 'tech quartet' of computers, tablets, smartphones and televisions will eventually deliver sustainable profits on the global stage. It is a far cry from the company that previously extolled an engineering-led narrative focused on subbrands such as Walkman and Trinitron.

Sir Howard predicted the need for major change some time ago. In a conversation two years before he moved to a nonexecutive role, he explained to me: 'The switch from analog to digital [technologies] mirrors the shift that corporations have to make. Mature companies – like mature industrial countries – have to have the imagination and vision to make another great leap forward. They have to recognize that markets such as Brazil, Russia, India and China represent new opportunities. Everybody knows this is a turning point.'

The problem for companies such as Sony is that other more nimble rivals have created more compelling narratives, or they have emerged unscathed by the sort of challenges battering the Japanese giant. Apple, in many ways Sony's nemesis, has not had to deal with the multiple challenges of a conservative workforce reluctant to shed the old ways of doing business, let alone the threats posed by an overvalued yen, aggressive online pirates, an earthquake and product recalls. Nor does Apple have to transform itself across multiple business divisions ranging from cameras to recorded music, from batteries to film production, or from TV distribution to video gaming.

While Sony has tried to tackle these myriad issues, Apple has forged ahead with a simple narrative. Tim Cook, who succeeded Steve Jobs as Apple chief executive shortly before the founder's untimely death in 2011, summarised the US company's core purpose on an analysts' call in 2009.

'We believe that we are on the face of the earth to make great products, and that's not changing. We are constantly focusing on innovating. We believe in the simple not the complex,' said Cook.

We believe that we need to own and control the primary technologies behind the products that we make, and participate only in markets where we can make a significant contribution. We believe in saying no to thousands of projects, so that we can really focus on the few that are truly important and meaningful to us. We believe in deep collaboration and cross-pollination of our groups, which allows us to innovate in a way that others cannot. And frankly, we don't settle for anything less than excellence in every group in the company, and we have the self-honesty to admit when we're wrong and the courage to change. And I think, regardless of who is in what job, those values are so embedded in this company that Apple will do extremely well.[29]

Apple can justify such broad brush statements given its product-led growth story, which saw it overtake Exxon Mobil to become the world's most valuable company in 2011. That year, the underlying strength of the business was further demonstrated when Apple's balance sheet revealed it had more cash than the US government.

Few other corporations have such a straightforward narrative. Instead, companies in industries from financial services to fast-moving consumer goods, or from car-making to healthcare, are struggling to articulate a clear vision of either existing strategy or future ambitions. Public relations agencies, sensing a business opportunity, are only too willing to test and revise their narratives. Such assignments have stimulated a growing PR capability in corporate reputation auditing and stakeholder analysis.

Amid a wave of marketing hype, one leading agency promises to 'measure the resonance of messages and provide an early warning system to flag potential issues'. Another offers 'issue mapping' to determine which core issues a company should be

---

[29] Tim Cook, Apple's earnings conference call, January 2009 http://www. macrumors.com/2009/01/22/tim-cooks-view-of-the-apple-philosophy/

engaged in and to identify stakeholder communities concerned with those same areas.

An ability to reshape client narratives may generate much-needed project revenues for PR firms. But the quality and efficacy of those narratives is harder to prove. The jury is out, for example, on whether Unilever derives much credit from its so-called 'sustainable living plan' – a commitment to increasing its social impact and decreasing the group's environmental footprint. Nor is it clear how much Marks & Spencer benefits from its 'Plan A' corporate responsibility programme, which chief executive Marc Bolland calls a model for sustainable consumption.

Advocates of such initiatives claim they are not optional in today's business environment. The company without a sustainability programme is deemed reputationally vulnerable. Yet, at many companies there is still significant internal resistance to the idea of a new narrative emphasising sustainable conduct, particularly given external scepticism about idealistic claims.

Any narrative that promises more than it delivers creates an obvious reputation risk when things go wrong. And it is often the PR function – the in-house team and their outside advisers – that carries the can when a narrative proves illusory, such as BP's much-derided 'Beyond Petroleum'. It is the PR team that has to explain to a sceptical media why a narrative was developed in the first place, while avoiding any disclosure of the costs involved and playing down criticism of management.

'Beyond Petroleum' was a classic case of a broken narrative. It demonstrated that a company should only extol such virtues when it has the financial track record, the product pipeline and potential growth opportunities to justify that sort of storyline. Even in the rare cases where such claims are justified, the benefits of a narrative can be undermined by weak or woolly language.

Fuzzy objectives, poorly expressed, are symptomatic of bad strategy, according to UCLA Management Professor Richard Rumelt.

He warns that corporate narratives run the risk of restating the obvious, especially when they include a generous sprinkling of buzzwords that masquerade as expertise. In short, a fluffy narrative is a hallmark of mediocrity.

Professor Rumelt maintains they are usually the product of a long list of things to do, often mis-labelled as strategies or objectives. In the *McKinsey Quarterly* of June 2011, he argues:

> Such lists usually grow out of planning meetings in which a wide variety of stakeholders suggest things that they would like to see accomplished. Rather than focus on a few important items, the group sweeps the whole day's collection into the strategic plan. Then, in recognition that it is a dog's dinner, the label 'long-term' is added, implying that none of these things need to be done today...
>
> A second type of weak strategic objective [or narrative] is one that is blue sky – typically a simple restatement of the desired state of affairs or of the challenge. It skips over the annoying fact that no one has a clue as to how to get there. A leader may successfully identify the key challenge and propose an overall approach to dealing with the challenge. But if the consequent strategic objectives are just as difficult to meet as the original challenge, the strategy has added little value.
>
> Good strategy, in contrast, works by focusing energy and resources on one, or a very few, pivotal objectives whose accomplishment will lead to a cascade of favorable outcomes. It also builds a bridge between the critical challenge at the heart of the strategy and action – between desire and immediate objectives that lie within grasp.

The problem for many companies and their PR advisers is that there is little external appetite for over-ambitious vision statements in today's business climate of volatile consumer demand and widespread public sector austerity. Additionally, the immediacy of internet verdicts has dramatically reduced the time and ability to defend a business narrative. This is creating a PR paradox: companies are desperate for a good reputation; they all want narratives that explain their virtues and that differentiate them from their peers. But simultaneously, there is less tolerance in the digital age for the manner in which companies describe themselves.

These narratives are being tested not only against companies' own performance, but also against the macroeconomic trends shaping global business.

Sir Martin Sorrell, chief executive of the marketing services giant WPP, believes there are nine big trends that businesses and their advisers must heed. First of all, he warns that globalisation will continue to drive business activity – particularly in a 'new G8' comprising the BRIC countries of Brazil, Russia, India and China alongside the 'MIST' countries: Mexico, Indonesia, South Korea and Turkey. The globalisation narrative is coupled to a second theme of worldwide overcapacity, encapsulated by the car industry where there is installed capacity to make 80 million vehicles a year while consumer demand is around 60 million.

The third big narrative is the continued encroachment of all things digital, with many executives describing the last 25 years of technology as just the warm-up act for a complete transformation of human interactivity. Any company without a narrative that includes a significant digital competence will be challenged. Addressing business leaders at an industry conference in London on 19 January 2012, Sir Martin explained that the fourth megatrend was the intensifying pressure between retailers and manufacturers in a low inflation, high technology market to deliver goods that remain relevant to consumers. In fifth place, he said that internal communications had to improve in the business world, with chairmen and chief executives facing growing calls to explain their strategies to worried internal audiences.

'My sixth point is that while there is significant global focus in business, there is also a switch to localism in relation to government, R&D and corporate social responsibility,' according to the WPP chief executive. Companies must be global in scale but local to touch, he argues. 'China is a country of 1.3 billion people and 32 provinces. It can't be covered by one country or regional manager.'

His last three narrative trends emphasised the absence of inflation, forcing companies to fight on costs rather than pricing. At the same time, the business world had to compete for attention with governments trying to market their rescue packages and stimulation plans. And lastly he warned that every company had to embrace corporate social responsibility at the heart of what they do.

These market forces are now affecting the PR industry. Agencies have to provide a compelling narrative for their clients in a fast-changing macro-marketplace, while also trying to win credit for a series of micro-messages that demonstrate some degree of corporate resilience. This represents a major change for firms that grew up as simple information brokers for the print media. Many of them are finding it difficult to persuade their clients and often their own employees that this is a type of consultancy suited to public relations. It is an ever harder change of direction for firms without a global outlook or a deep resource of industry intelligence. At the most basic level, the PR industry cannot hope to reboot their client narratives if they themselves cannot articulate why it's necessary, or if they fail to identify the main issues that worry leading companies.

Of all the macro-trends reshaping the business world, the European Roundtable of Industrialists has decided that one overriding issue should inform corporate narratives. At a council meeting on 9 December 2011, the forum of around 45 chairmen and chief executives of large European companies warned:

'All policies across Europe must aim to improve industrial competitiveness. For too long, competitiveness has been seen as one out of many policy objectives. But if we are not competitive, we will not come out of the crisis and will be unable to achieve any of our other objectives. Improving competitiveness must really be the main objective of all policies at all levels.'

Clearly, an uncompetitive company will always struggle to develop a compelling narrative or a positive reputation. Should companies care? After all, a good reputation and a coherent narrative are intangible assets; neither contributes directly to the bottom line. But the costs of ignoring your reputation can be high.

A senior executive at one of the world's leading industrial companies admits that it deliberately 'suppressed its narrative' while undergoing a major restructuring. The company told its PR advisers that there was no upside in telling its broader story while trying to repair its balance sheet. The company, which suffered a major identity crisis during its overhaul, decided to revisit the narrative issue only once it had returned to profitability. 'We went quiet for five years while we fixed the business,' the executive recalls. 'And then we decided – let's construct a corporate narrative that unites people behind where we're going. We needed an aspirational picture of what we wanted to be.'

By the time the company was ready to talk again it found that the world had changed. Rivals had exploited its absence to portray themselves as the technology leaders or global market champions of their industry. New players had emerged from both the BRIC and MIST countries to fight for customers. And the media, itself seeking a narrative for the digital world, was unwilling to give the company the benefit of the doubt. 'We asked our PR advisers what was going on,' adds the executive, a member of the global management committee. 'They told us to prepare for the worst. The old rules of engagement had changed.'

CHAPTER 21

New Rules of Engagement

Gary Ginsberg was angry. The head of communications at News Corporation, for many years Rupert Murdoch's gate-keeper, had taken exception to the *FT*'s handling of the media giant's quarterly earnings.

As the *FT*'s media editor approached his glass-walled office for a peace-meeting, Ginsberg picked up a baseball bat and practised a few theatrical swings. The message was clear: don't cross me again. At the time, Ginsberg was the point man for all information going in and out of the company.

Michael Wolff, the media commentator and columnist for *Vanity Fair*, says Ginsberg's job was to protect Murdoch from himself, 'or to protect News Corp from its worst and basest impulses'. Wolff adds:

> Everybody confers with Ginsberg about what the old man is thinking – not least of all because the old man doesn't necessarily ever say what he's thinking, or say what he's thinking to any one person in any consistent way – and if he does, he mumbles so much, and his accent is so thick, that you might not understand him anyway. Everybody tends to have just their piece of the story – Ginsberg pieces together the pieces.[30]

Or at least they used to; Ginsberg left News Corp before the phone-hacking scandal in Britain swept over the company – forcing the media group to jettison numerous executives, and derailing the assumed succession plan: for James Murdoch to step into his father's shoes. The absence of the company's most effective communicator was keenly felt at News Corp's

---

[30] Michael Wolff, *The Man who Owns the News*, London, Bodley Head, 2008.

Manhattan headquarters. His departure, for a bigger role at arch-rival Time Warner, presaged a loss of reputation control just as the company was about to face a PR disaster.

The subsequent mauling of News Corp, particularly by the anti-Murdoch media in Britain and Australia, has been a test case for a wider breakdown in corporate public relations. A media pack unleashed, sensing executive blood, has seized on every revelation, relished every leak and damned the company before any of the judicial and regulatory inquiries have been completed. News Corp insiders have been particularly incensed by the wall-to-wall coverage in *The Guardian*, the left-leaning newspaper, which they accuse of 'indulging in the longest victory lap in media history'.

Its triumphalism reached new levels in 2012 after Rupert Murdoch, acknowledging criticism in a UK parliamentary report, told employees in an internal memo: 'We certainly should have acted more quickly and aggressively to uncover wrongdoing. We deeply regret what took place and have taken our share of responsibility for not rectifying the situation sooner.'

Whatever the rights and wrongs at News Corp – and a lot went wrong – one of the side-effects has been to shine an uncompromising light on the efficacy of business PR. Coming hot on the heels of other corporate crises, News Corp has become the latest high-profile brand to suffer a reputation meltdown and loss of trust. The communications strategy of its UK newspaper subsidiary, the source of the scandal, seemed based on containment, denial and obfuscation.

Once that PR edifice started to crumble, it exposed a company wrought by infighting and non-disclosure among its senior executives and editorial staff. The self-inflicted problems at News International have reinforced a widely held suspicion in broader society that large companies have a problem with telling the truth about their activities.

Even before the latest allegations of misconduct, a Harris Interactive Poll found that almost 90 per cent of respondents judged corporate reputation at a ten-year low. In its latest survey of 60 leading companies, Harris Interactive reported that just eight businesses were judged to have excellent reputations – down 50 per cent on the findings in 2011. 'With the erosion of trust in corporate leadership, consumers have high expectations and are demanding more information and transparency from companies with which they plan to spend their hard earned dollars,' according to Harris.[31]

The findings represent a major challenge to the $10 billion-a-year market for public relations. It is an industry at a crossroads – facing shifting client demands, a contraction in lucrative transaction mandates, downward pressure on fees, combined with calls for greater regulation and disclosure – all exacerbated by eroding media standards and the disruption of the world's evolving digital ecosystem. Of those many challenges, the immediacy of the internet has posed arguably the greatest threat to old school PR manipulation. Traditional powers of persuasion, targeted mainly at print media, have been undermined by the explosion in online commentary on multiple content devices.

'Our greatest challenge today is deciding where to begin telling a story,' Richard Edelman, leader of the agency that bears his name, told the Institute of Public Relations in his address, 'Reimagining our Profession: Public Relations for a Complex World', on 10 November 2011.

There are four distinct, but related, types of media today: mainstream, hybrid, social, and owned. Imagine them as a four-leaf clover. In the first leaf, mainstream, we have the traditional delivery vehicles of print or broadcast. In the second leaf, hybrid, are the dot.com versions of traditional media and media that is born

---

[31] www.harrisinteractive.com

digital like the Huffington Post. The third leaf, social, includes Facebook, Twitter feeds and YouTube channels. The fourth leaf, owned, includes a brand or company's websites and apps – vitally important because every company should be a media company.

Sitting in the middle of the clover is search, the new on-ramp to all forms of media, as well as content which fuels search rank.

And there are also new influencers, such as the 25,000 people who provide half the world's tweets. They're passionate, fast, and prolific, which makes their expertise and personal experience resonate globally.

Digital proliferation creates both challenges and opportunities throughout the information marketplace. PR companies are, with varying degrees of success, trying to navigate all types of social media. Reputation managers now have more routes through which to distribute positive messages. But it is almost impossible to choreograph the proliferation of digital news, much of it disposable in nature.

If social media is causing unease among PR practitioners, it is creating a thinly veiled panic for their traditional counterparts: print and broadcast media. Analogue news outlets in mature markets around the world are looking nervously over their shoulders at the free-for-all journalism practised by bloggers, Twitter users and online aggregators. The unintended consequence of online technology has been to create an information tornado, flinging aside the normal rules of engagement on accuracy, regulation, trust, context and redress.

The media has been tossed about in this whirlwind. Newspaper circulation and television viewing are in structural decline. Newsrooms are cutting budgets, staff, pagination and broadcast news. In North America alone, print advertising has declined more than 20 per cent since 2011 while print subscriptions have also suffered double-digit declines, cutting total print and digital revenues in the newspaper industry from $36.4 billion to $32 billion.[32]

Newspaper owners have taken some comfort from rising digital consumption and increasing mobile traffic. Yet the internet has also created a media problem: more mouths (or screens) to feed with fewer resources. Hence, the pressure on news media to produce revelatory stories has never been greater, including a voracious appetite for the 'fall from grace' corporate scoop.

In this swirling ultra-competitive environment, the media is often unwilling to take PR guidance at face value. Reporters are more willing to take risks in pursuit of a 'gotcha' story. The ensuing turbulence has upset traditional PR practices. Agencies can no longer promise their clients a high degree of media management. Clients in turn are increasingly disenchanted with paying hefty retainers for what they regard as passive communications insurance, with no guarantee of positive results when a crisis breaks. The loss of control has only been exacerbated by globalisation, in which a company's discomfort in one market can spread virally to every territory in which it operates – at the click of a blogger's send button.

The risk culture is not confined to journalism. PR agencies have been accused of resorting to desperate measures to defend client reputations, including manipulating search rankings or altering Wikipedia entries. The pressure to deliver results and, in the most extreme cases, launder the reputations of unsavoury clients has intensified. Media scrutiny of such practices has made a number of PR and political lobbying firms the one thing they don't want to be: front-page news, rather than mere messengers.

Leading players in the public relations and lobbying community argue emphatically that these are two different businesses, where evidence of bad behaviour in one stream should not be used to condemn the other. One thing is true: public

---

[32] www.generatorresearch.com

relations is focused mainly on the downstream business of securing favourable coverage and positive external perceptions of an agency's clients. Political and business lobbying is focused on the upstream, behind-the-scenes, engagement with politicians, regulators and international organisations to educate such opinion formers about a client's interests.

Lord Bell, a seasoned practitioner of both PR and lobbying, said in an interview on BBC *Newsnight* on 3 April 2012: 'We are effectively messengers, what we do is devise strategy. We talk about the methodology of the way things work. We talk about the opportunity that people have to change things if they don't like the way they are going and we advise them on who they should talk to.'

That catch-all description underlines the growing convergence of the strategic communications industry. In spite of disagreements between different practitioners, the activities of lobbyists, financial PR firms, intelligence agencies, product marketing and management consultancy are coalescing under the broad umbrella of reputation.

In the eyes of most members of the public there is little difference between the various applications of reputation management. And calls are getting louder for greater transparency about the excesses of the 'dark arts'.

In Britain, the growing controversy over lobbying practices has prompted demands for greater compliance, independent regulation and a register of clients and their interests. If imposed, such rules will hasten the demise of the old feudal structure, the system of patronage by which business leaders distributed mandates to favoured PR and public affairs agencies, confident that they could manage client profiles with a few well-placed calls to senior journalists or friendly politicians. This cheerfully amateur model, with its roots in the world of gentlemen's clubs, has been cruelly exposed by the wave of corporate crises that began with the 2008 financial turmoil, and which has continued to claim corporate victims.

'The events of the last two years put risk-related issues squarely on the corporate boards' front burner, and the flame remains high,' according to Peter Brabeck-Letmathe, chairman of Nestlé, in *Calculated Risk?*, a 2011 report by the Korn/Ferry Institute. 'Board members are proactively rethinking their approach to risk, asking: How does risk inform our corporate strategy?'

Similar rethinks are taking place across the business community, including among advisers and the external audiences – notably the media – that they seek to influence. A new approach to communications and risk management may be a sign of acceptance, finally, to the changed order by which companies and their agents disclose information. It follows a long period of introspection, which has seen many corporations work through the stages of grief of denial, anger, bargaining and depression before accepting their altered reputation.

In a world of increased scrutiny, compliance and transparency, such companies and their retained PR advisers must communicate more professionally. Effective communications requires clear and concise messaging that is honest and based on reality, especially in a business environment of short attention spans, media risk-taking and public scepticism. In its June 2009 *Quarterly*, McKinsey, the consultancy firm that has suffered its own profile problems, maintains: 'Reputations are built on a foundation not only of communications but also of deeds: stakeholders can see through PR that isn't supported by real and consistent business activity.'

For far too long, many companies regarded reputation as a consequence of their day-to-day operations and services. But recent crises have forced a redefinition to include reputation based on how a company behaves, how it deals with specific problems; whether it has integrity, whether it deserves trust. This redefined landscape is forcing a painful readjustment in the PR industry. Firms that previously owned the whole area of external communications are now finding themselves competing in a converged reputation marketplace with all manner of other advisers. In the new reputation economy, it is harder to secure the guaranteed fees, the quality of staff and to produce the positive outcomes expected by clients.

A similar reappraisal is underway among the clients themselves, with previously distinct and often aggressively territorial corporate departments being forced to work together in the interests of reputation management. Nir Kossovsky, chief executive of Steel City Re, one of the new phalanx of reputation management firms, says in *Intellectual Asset Management* magazine for May/June 2011:

> A number of companies operate with a fully integrated communications platform. Others lack even the most basic elements, such as a corporate image book, set of language standards and other elements of communication. Communications silos in the areas of product marketing, investor relations and corporate communication are sources of messaging risk and therefore enterprise value risk.

Across industry, the heightened awareness of risk is changing attitudes towards corporate reputation. Business organisations are recommending that reputation should form part of every organisation's risk register so that potential threats can be identified, prioritised and planned for. Beyond such compliance measures, it is clear that boards should be trained in reputation management skills – or at least their competence audited – and that a reputation test should be applied in future to decision-making about product planning, international expansion, corporate governance, remuneration and potential transactions. Companies should conduct similar tests on how they express their personality and vision, as well as which distribution tools and online platforms – and which advisers – are used to reach various stakeholders.

The public relations industry is uncertain exactly where it fits in to this evolving business climate. Corporate clients are unsure how best to use their PR advisers, and how to reward them with different sorts of mandates.

Leading PR agencies, ranging from bulge-bracket firms such as Hill & Knowlton, Burson Marstellar and Edelman, through to mid-size outfits including Brunswick of the UK or Kekst in the USA, and the long tail of small boutiques, are all determined to survive and thrive in the market for crisis management and corporate reputation. They insist that they will remain necessary adjuncts to corporate clients large and small, contributing strategic counsel, risk awareness and media engagement capabilities that are now more relevant than ever. They promise to do so by applying new digital capabilities, international reach and old-style powers of persuasion. Somewhat reluctantly, their leadership teams are now learning the language of trust and reputation management, reflecting the sensitivities of increasingly worried clients.

The reputation lexicon is also being adopted by in-house PR leaders, all of them conscious of increased vulnerability. As the communications chief of one US financial services institution says: 'Is there a more valued commodity in business than reputation? Is there a value harder – and easier – to lose? Further, while reputation and trust used to be established solely through a product's effectiveness, maintaining trust today is much more complex. It intertwines product, regulatory, community, customer experience, communications and more.'

Mindful that companies need outside advice to manage their reputation, he adds: 'A strategic communications firm must manage the thoughtful balance of offence and defence: advise and execute on how to gently advance the case of trust, while being continually mindful to protect the downside. Any overreach could backfire; any failure to anticipate potential negatives can mean ruin.'

The crises of recent years have propelled the broad issue of reputation to the top of the business agenda. Having watched other companies crash and burn, businesses are well aware of how precarious they are. They are conscious that the media, in all its forms, is in no mood for forgiveness. Scepticism in the media is widely shared by regulators, politicians, competitors, employees, suppliers and ultimately – and most importantly – customers. There is no tolerance any more, if it ever existed, for spin or artifice in public relations. Communications must be honest, transparent and based on facts. The practice of 'dark arts' may be coming to an end.

The impetus towards honest dialogue signals a return to the founding principles of public relations. Whether working in-house or for outside advisers, PR practitioners should deliver truthful messages that satisfy expectations among multiple audiences. In spite of today's complex digital ecosystem, those expectations remain broadly the same as when Edward Bernays laid the first ground rules of PR in the 1920s. Back then, as today, people prefer companies they trust. He wrote:

> Just as the production manager must be familiar with every element in detail concerning the materials with which he is working, so the man in charge of the firm's public relations must be familiar with the structure, the prejudices, and the whims of the general public, and must handle his problems with the utmost care. The public has its own standards and demands and habits. You may modify them, but you dare not run counter to them.'[33]

Setting the standard for the PR industry of the twentieth century, and the direction it should pursue in the twenty-first, the father of public relations added:

---

[33] E.L. Bernays, *Propaganda*, New York, Ig Publishing, 2004.

Both business and the public have their own person-
alities which must somehow be brought into friendly
agreement. Conflict and suspicion are injurious to both.
Modern business must study on what terms the partnership can be made amicable and mutually beneficial. It
must explain itself, its aims, its objectives, to the public
in terms which the public can understand and is willing
to accept.

INDEX